Sea Creatures

Written by Jen Green
Illustrated by Michael Posen

p

This is a Parragon Book
First published in 2000

Parragon
Queen Street House
4 Queen Street
Bath BA1 1HE, UK

ISBN 0-75253-502-1

Printed in Dubai, U.A.E

Produced by
Monkey Puzzle Media Ltd
Gissing's Farm
Fressingfield
Suffolk IP21 5SH
UK

Designer: Sarah Crouch
Cover design: Victoria Webb
Editor: Linda Sonntag
Artwork commissioning: Roger Goddard-Coote
Project manager: Alex Edmonds

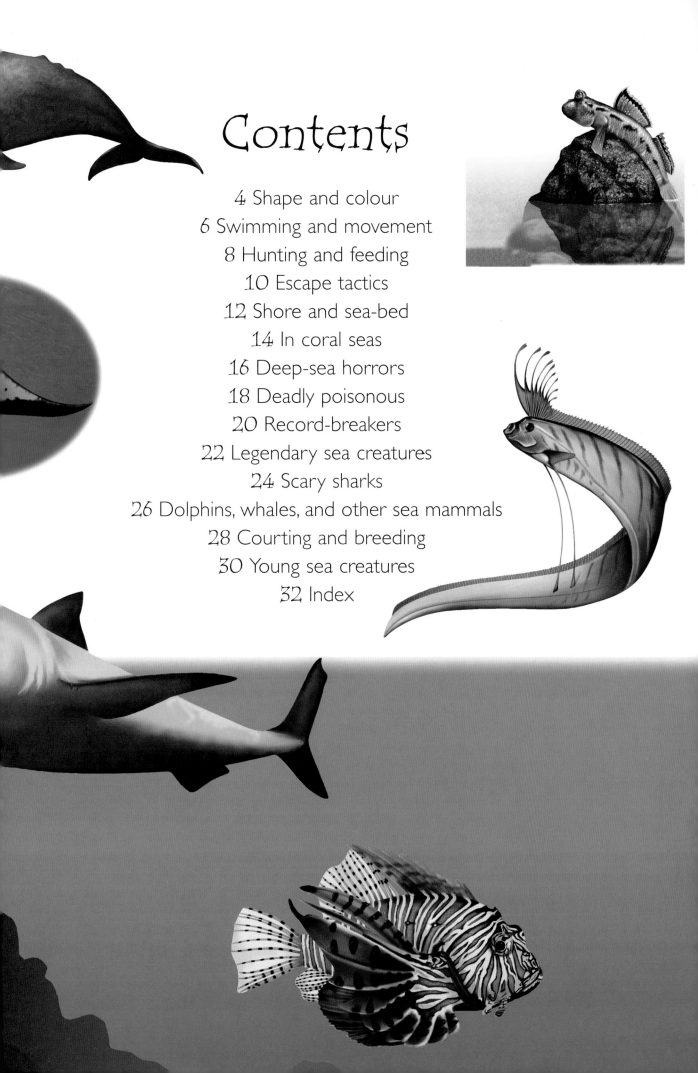

Contents

Why do most fish have slim, tapering bodies?

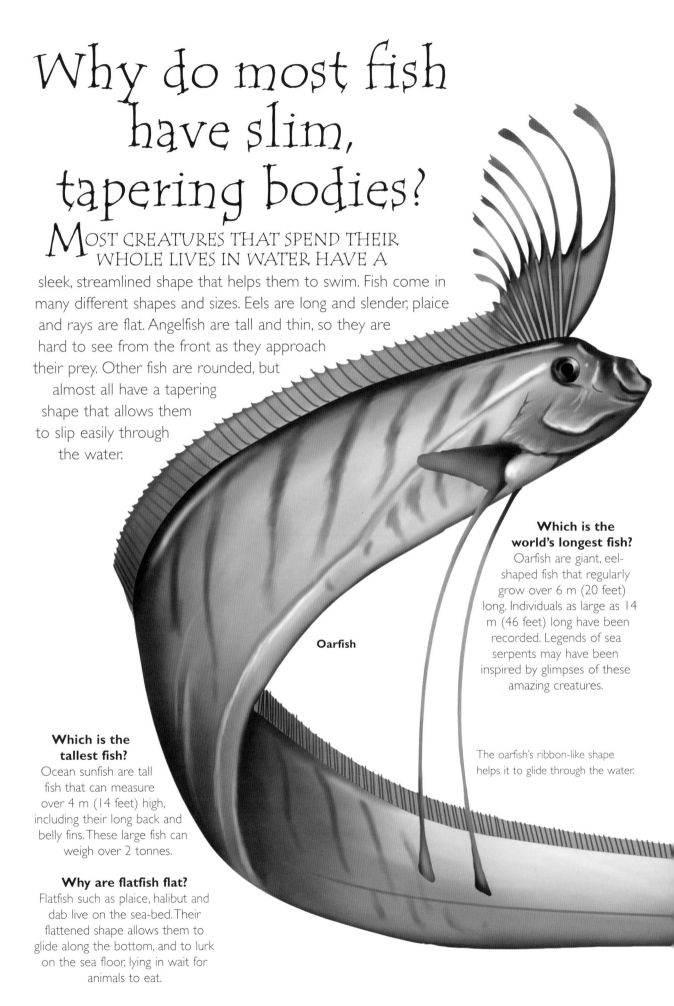

MOST CREATURES THAT SPEND THEIR WHOLE LIVES IN WATER HAVE A sleek, streamlined shape that helps them to swim. Fish come in many different shapes and sizes. Eels are long and slender, plaice and rays are flat. Angelfish are tall and thin, so they are hard to see from the front as they approach their prey. Other fish are rounded, but almost all have a tapering shape that allows them to slip easily through the water.

Oarfish

Which is the world's longest fish?

Oarfish are giant, eel-shaped fish that regularly grow over 6 m (20 feet) long. Individuals as large as 14 m (46 feet) long have been recorded. Legends of sea serpents may have been inspired by glimpses of these amazing creatures.

The oarfish's ribbon-like shape helps it to glide through the water.

Which is the tallest fish?

Ocean sunfish are tall fish that can measure over 4 m (14 feet) high, including their long back and belly fins. These large fish can weigh over 2 tonnes.

Why are flatfish flat?

Flatfish such as plaice, halibut and dab live on the sea-bed. Their flattened shape allows them to glide along the bottom, and to lurk on the sea floor, lying in wait for animals to eat.

How do fish hide in the open sea?

Herring, mackerel and many other fish that swim near the surface of the great oceans have dark backs and pale bellies. This colouring, called countershading, works to cancel out the effect of sunlight shining on their bodies from above, and so helps these fish to hide even in open water.

What creatures plant a garden on their backs?

Spider crabs make their own disguises from materials they find in the sea around them. They clip living sponges or fronds of seaweed with their strong pincers, and plant them on their backs. When the seaweed dies, they replace it with a fresh piece!

Why do some fish have bright colours?

Many fish that live in tropical seas are brightly coloured or marked with bold spots and patterns. This colouring helps them to hide among the brightly coloured coral and dark shadows, but also helps them to stand out clearly in open water. In the breeding season, when these fish are seeking mates and want to be noticed, they swim out into the open and become very obvious.

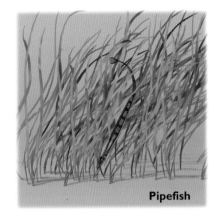

Pipefish

Predators find it very difficult to spot pipefish hiding among strands of seaweed.

What fish looks like seaweed?

Pipefish are long, slim, dark green fish that look just like strands of seaweed. In shallow, weedy waters, they swim upright among the seaweed fronds, and resemble their surroundings so closely that they are almost impossible to see.

Carpet shark

The carpet shark's camouflage helps to conceal it from its prey.

How does the carpet shark stay hidden?

Many sea creatures have bodies with colours, shapes and patterns that blend in with their surroundings. This natural disguise, or camouflage, helps them to hide from enemies or sneak up on their prey. Carpet sharks live and hunt on the sea-bed. Their pale, blotchy colours help hide them from their prey – small fish and crabs – as they lie motionless on the bottom.

Flying fish leap up to 2 m (6 feet) in the air, and glide along with outstretched fins.

What sea creature looks like a pair of false teeth?

Scallops have a hard, hinged shell to protect their soft bodies. Some kinds of scallop swim along by clapping the two halves of their shell together so water shoots out of the back. The swimming scallop looks like a pair of false teeth chattering as it zips along!

Which fish is the fastest swimmer?

Sailfish are large hunting fish that live in the open ocean. With their long, streamlined snouts, torpedo-shaped bodies and powerful tails, they can speed along at up to 109 kph (67 mph).

Which sea creature is the deepest diver?

Sperm whales are expert divers. Like all whales, they breathe at the surface, but swim down to depths of 500 m (1,600 feet) to hunt deep-sea creatures such as giant squid. The snouts of sperm whales often bear the scars of battles with the squid.

How do fish swim?

Most fish swim by arching their bodies and swishing their tails from side to side. The fish's body and tail push against the water to propel it forwards. The chest, back and belly fins help with steering and braking. A gas-filled organ called the swim bladder keeps the fish buoyant in the water.

Which sea creature uses jet-propulsion?

The octopus has a funnel-shaped siphon sticking out from its body. It shoots a jet of water from the funnel to propel itself along, and can point its siphon in different directions to steer.

Which fish "flies" underwater?

Rays are flattened fish that live near the sea-bed. They swim along by flapping their wide, flat chest fins like wings, so they look as if they are flying underwater.

Which fish flies through the air?

Flying fish take to the air to escape from hungry predators such as sailfish and marlins. The flying fish gets up speed, then leaps right out of the water. In the air, it spreads its chest fins so they act like wings, keeping the fish airborne for up to 100 m (325 feet).

Mudskippers survive on land by filling their large gill-chambers with water.

How do jellyfish get about?

Jellyfish are soft creatures with bodies shaped like bells or saucers. To get about, they contract their bag-like bodies so water shoots out behind, pushing the creature along.

Which fish can walk on land?

Mudskippers are fish that live in swamps and muddy estuaries on tropical coasts. They come right out of the water and scurry about on land, using their muscular chest fins as crutches.

Why do dolphins leap out of the water?

DOLPHINS AND WHALES HAVE TAILS THAT ARE FLATTENED HORIZONTALLY, not vertically like fish-tails. They swim by sweeping their tails up and down. When swimming at speed, dolphins leap out of the water to save energy, because is is quicker and easier to move through air than water. Like all water-dwelling mammals, dolphins must also surface to breathe.

Mudskipper

How do barracuda surprise their prey?

The barracuda is a fierce hunting fish of tropical seas. It has keen eyesight and is armed with razor-sharp teeth. Its blue-grey colouring blends in well with the ocean, allowing it to sneak up on a shoal of small fish. The hunter speeds into the middle of the shoal with its jaws snapping, and seizes its prey in its deadly teeth.

How does the anemone catch its dinner?

Sea anemones are armed with a crown of stinging tentacles. When small fish brush against them, the stings fire and release a paralysing poison. Then the tentacles push the weakened prey into the anemone's mouth.

Which fish has a fishing rod?

THE ANGLERFISH HAS A BUILT-IN FISHING ROD ON ITS HEAD – A LONG, THIN spine with a fleshy lobe on the end that looks like a wiggling worm. The angler lurks on the sea-bed, squat-bodied and well-camouflaged. When a small crab comes up to eat the "worm", the anglerfish lunges forward and grabs its prey in its enormous mouth.

Which fish has a secret weapon?

The torpedo ray. It can generate electricity using special muscles in its head. The ray lurks on the sea-bed, waiting for small fish to pounce on. It wraps its fins around its victims and blasts them with a charge of 200 volts.

The anglerfish lures its prey with its built-in fishing rod, complete with bait.

Archerfish start to shoot water when they are young, but only the adults can aim well enough to hit their target.

Archerfish

Which fish runs a cleaning service?

SMALL FISH CALLED CLEANER WRASSE

feed on parasites that infest larger fish. The big fish welcome this cleaning service, so do not harm the wrasse, even when it swims right inside a big fish's mouth to clean. Sometimes queues of fish form at the wrasse's cleaning station, patiently waiting their turn for a "wash and brush-up".

Which fish shoots to kill?

On tropical sea coasts, skilled archerfish can catch prey such as spiders that are perched on plants overhanging the water. With their powerful lips, they squirt a jet of water at their target and knock their prey into the water.

Anglerfish

How do parrotfish eat their meals?

Parrotfish have hard mouths shaped like parrots' beaks. With their tough mouths they scrape algae and coral from the rocks. This food is then ground to a powder by horny plates inside the fish's mouth.

What fish is a thirsty bloodsucker?

Lampreys are strange fish with eel-shaped bodies. Instead of jaws, they have round mouths filled with rows of horny teeth. The lamprey uses its mouth as a sucker to fasten on to another fish's body. Its teeth scrape away the fish's skin, then the lamprey drinks its blood!

What creature gives a nasty nip?

Porcupine fish

CRABS AND THEIR RELATIVES, LOBSTERS, BELONG TO A GROUP OF shelled creatures called crustaceans. The crab's soft body parts are protected by a hard outer case that forms a snug suit of armour. The creature is also armed with powerful claws that can give a nasty nip if an enemy comes too close.

How do herring avoid being eaten?
Fish such as herring and mackerel swim in groups called shoals. Living in a large group provides safety in numbers, because it is difficult for predators to single out a likely target among a shifting, shimmering mass of fish.

What is slimy and hides in anemones?
In tropical seas, clownfish hide from their enemies among the stinging tentacles of sea anemones. The tentacles do not harm the clownfish because its body is covered with a thick layer of slimy mucus, but no predator dares to come close!

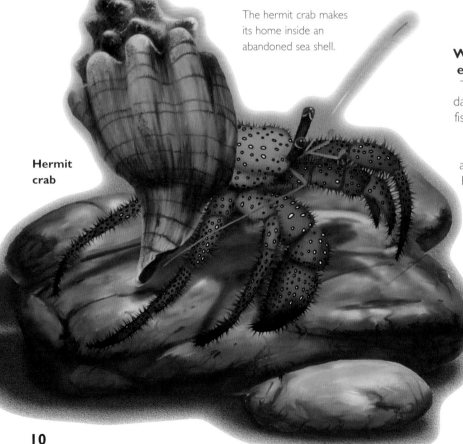

The hermit crab makes its home inside an abandoned sea shell.

Hermit crab

Which fish makes eyes at its enemies?
The twinspot wrasse has two dark patches on its back. Hunting fish may mistake the spots for the eyes of a large and possibly dangerous creature, and swim away. If this trick fails, the wrasse has another. It dives down to the sea-bed and quickly buries itself in the sand.

Why does the hermit crab need a home?
Unlike other crabs, the hermit crab has no hard case to protect it. Instead, it shelters its soft rear end inside an empty sea shell. As the crab grows bigger, its shell becomes too tight, so it moves into a larger new home.

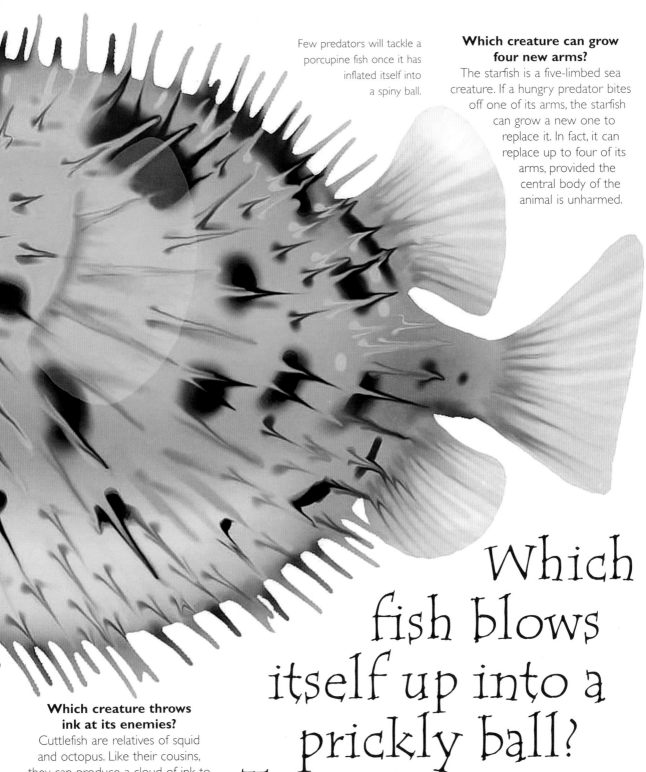

Few predators will tackle a porcupine fish once it has inflated itself into a spiny ball.

Which creature can grow four new arms?

The starfish is a five-limbed sea creature. If a hungry predator bites off one of its arms, the starfish can grow a new one to replace it. In fact, it can replace up to four of its arms, provided the central body of the animal is unharmed.

Which creature throws ink at its enemies?

Cuttlefish are relatives of squid and octopus. Like their cousins, they can produce a cloud of ink to confuse their enemies. The cuttlefish jets away under cover of this "smokescreen".

What makes a pistol shrimp go bang?

Pistol shrimps are named after the cracking noise they make by snapping their claws. Enemies are frightened off by these unexpected "pistol shots".

Which fish blows itself up into a prickly ball?

THE PORCUPINE FISH IS NAMED FOR THE SHARP SPINES, LIKE A PORCUPINE'S, that cover its body. Usually the spines lie flat against the fish's body, but if danger threatens, it can raise them. If an enemy comes too close, the fish takes in water so that its body swells to twice its normal size. It becomes a prickly ball too large and uncomfortable for predators to swallow. When the danger passes, the porcupine slowly returns to its normal shape and size.

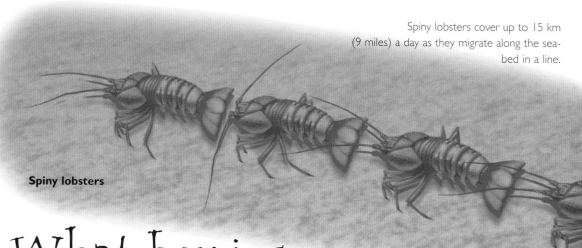

Spiny lobsters cover up to 15 km (9 miles) a day as they migrate along the sea-bed in a line.

Spiny lobsters

What buries itself in the sand?

Many creatures that dwell on the ocean bottom escape

from their enemies by burying themselves in the sand or mud. Crabs dig down and lie low with just their sensitive antennae showing. Weeverfish, which hide in the same way, have eyes on top of their heads. Their eyes stick out above the sand so the fish can still see while the rest of its body is buried.

Which fish "walks" on three legs?

The tripod fish is a strange fish that lives in deep, dark waters. Its two chest fins and tail fin have long, stiff spines. Together, the three spines form a tripod which the fish uses to rest and move along the sea-bed.

The tripod fish uses its stiff spines like stilts to walk along the sea-bed.

Tripod fish

How did the butterfish get its name?

Butterfish are long, slender fish that live in pools on rocky sea-shores. The slimy, slippery feel of their bodies has earned them their name.

How does a limpet grip its rock?

The limpet clamps its muscular foot on to a seaside rock and grips by suction. Even the pounding waves cannot dislodge it. Its hold is so tight it can be prised away only if an enemy attacks without warning.

Which creature has five sets of jaws?

Underneath its round, spiny body, the sea urchin has a mouth with five sets of jaws. It feeds by crawling along the sea floor, scraping seaweed and tiny creatures from the rocks.

Why do crabs walk sideways?

All crabs have ten legs – eight for walking and two with powerful pincers for picking up food. Crabs scuttle sideways along the shore and sea-bed. The sideways movement helps to prevent them tripping over their own legs! Large species of crab move only slowly, but small ghost crabs can scurry along the shore at a fast clip.

What queues up for its winter holiday?

Spiny lobsters live mainly solitary lives. But each year in autumn they gather to move to deeper waters where they will be safe from violent storms. The lobsters form a long line and march off along the sea-bed. When they reach their winter holiday destination they separate, and only meet up again to begin the long trip back.

Which fish would disappear on a chess board?

Plaice are flatfish that live on the sea-bed. In a matter of minutes, they can change their body colour from pale and sandy to dark or blotchy, to match their surroundings as they drift over the sea-bed in search of food. They can even adjust their colouring to become checkered if a chess board is placed under them! Only the upper part of the fish, visible to enemies, is coloured. The underside is white.

What needs a new suit of armour every year?

A crab's shell gives good protection. The disadvantage is that there is no space inside for the crab to grow! Each year, the crab sheds its old, tight skin and grows a new, slightly larger one. While the new soft skin is still hardening the creature is very easy to attack, so it hides away from enemies under rocks.

What is coral made of?

CORAL REEFS ARE MADE BY TINY CREATURES CALLED POLYPS

that live in colonies in tropical seas. Polyps are shaped like little sea anemones, but have a hard, chalky cup-shaped shell to protect their bodies. When they die, the shells remain, and new polyps grow on top of them. Over time, billions of shells build up to form a coral reef.

Surgeonfish

Where is the world's biggest coral reef?
The Great Barrier Reef off the north-east coast of Australia is the world's largest coral reef. Stretching for 2,000 km (1,200 miles), it is the largest structure made by living creatures. The reef is home to many spectacular animals, including 1,500 different kinds of fish.

What are dead man's fingers?
Dead man's fingers is a species of soft coral that grows on rocks. Each coral colony is made up of thousands of polyps that form a fleshy mass like a rubbery hand. When a piece of this coral washes up on the sea-shore, it may give swimmers a fright!

Why does a crown-of-thorns threaten coral reefs?
The crown-of-thorns starfish is a reef-killer. It fastens on to the living coral, sticks its stomach out, and releases juices that digest the coral polyps. When only the coral shells are left, the starfish moves on. It can kill a big patch of coral in a day, and has destroyed large areas of the Great Barrier Reef.

Leafy seadragon

Which fish has the head of a horse and the tail of a monkey?
The sea-horse is an unusual fish with a head shaped like the knight in a chess set. It holds its body upright and swims along by waving its back fins. It uses its long, curling tail to anchor itself in the seaweed while it searches for small creatures to eat. Its eyes can swivel independently, so the sea-horse can hunt for food and watch out for enemies at the same time!

The surgeonfish defends itself by lashing its tail, which is armed with razor-sharp blades.

What clams up in a hurry?
Giant clams live on the Great Barrier Reef. Their huge, hinged shells measure up to 1.5 m (5 feet) wide, and weigh 250 kg (550 lb). The giant clam generally has its shell open so it can feed, but if danger threatens, it can slam the two halves shut. Inquisitive sea creatures had better watch out!

Which fish can attack with a scalpel?
Surgeonfish of tropical seas have sharp little blades like scalpels at the base of their tails. Usually the bony blades lie flat against the fish's body, but they can be flicked out like knives if an enemy approaches.

What is a leafy seadragon?

The leafy seadragon is a large sea-horse that lives in warm Australian water. This creature is a master of disguise. Its body is covered with long, trailing flaps of skin that look like strands of seaweed. It is very difficult to spot as it swims among the weeds.

Ragged flaps of skin disguise the leafy seadragon as it drifts among the seaweed.

Hatchetfish

How do fish hide in dark seas?
Deep-sea fish are camouflaged to blend in with their surroundings. Many have black or dark bodies to match the inky waters. Others are transparent. Hatchetfish have silvery bodies that reflect any small gleams of light.

The hatchetfish has a line of tiny lights running down its belly that hides its shadow in the water.

What creatures can survive at great ocean depths?

Viperfish

A CENTURY AGO, SCIENTISTS BELIEVED THAT NO LIFE COULD EXIST in the very deep oceans. Now we know that creatures do survive there, but conditions are very harsh. A thousand metres (3,330 feet) below the sunlit surface, the water is pitch-black and very cold. Deep-sea fish must be able to stand the great pressure caused by the weight of water on top of them, which would kill surface creatures. Many deep-sea fish look like monsters from a horror film, with large heads, huge mouths with fierce teeth, and long, thin bodies. Yet most of these deep-sea horrors are very small – less than 30 cm (1 ft) long.

Why are deep-sea fish mysterious?

SCIENTISTS STILL KNOW VERY LITTLE ABOUT DEEP-SEA FISH, BECAUSE

of the difficulties of descending to the ocean bottom to study them. Most deep-sea fish don't survive if they are brought to the surface. Some even explode, because their bodies are built to withstand the great pressure of the ocean depths!

How do deep-sea creatures find their food in the dark?

In the black depths, many deep-sea fish sense their prey by smell, taste and touch. A line of nerves running down the fish's body picks up vibrations in the water caused by other swimming creatures. Some deep-sea hunters have long touch- and taste-sensitive tentacles trailing from their jaws.

Can deep-sea fish see in the dark?

For many deep-sea fish, vision is little use in the inky darkness. They have tiny eyes, or no eyes at all, and cannot see. Other fish have large eyes that pick up any faint glimmers of light, or tube-shaped eyes that work like binoculars. Still other species make their own light to hunt their prey.

Why don't gulper eels get hungry?

Food is scarce in the ocean depths, for no water plants and few creatures live there. So fishes' meals are few and far between. Gulper eels and viperfish have large, stretchy stomachs that can expand to fit any victim that passes. Another deep-sea fish, the black swallower, can swallow and digest a fish twice its own size.

With its giant mouth, the viperfish is a fierce deep-ocean predator. The long teeth point backwards to make sure no prey escapes from its jaws.

How do deep-sea creatures light up the dark?

As many as 1,000 different fish make light in the deep oceans. Some have luminous bacteria living under their skin. Others have special light-producing organs, or can cause a chemical reaction that gives off light.

What hunts with a luminous "worm"?

Like other anglerfish, the deep-sea angler has a long, thin spine that forms a "fishing rod" to catch prey creatures. On the end of the spine, a luminous lure dangles like a glowing worm to attract the fish's victims.

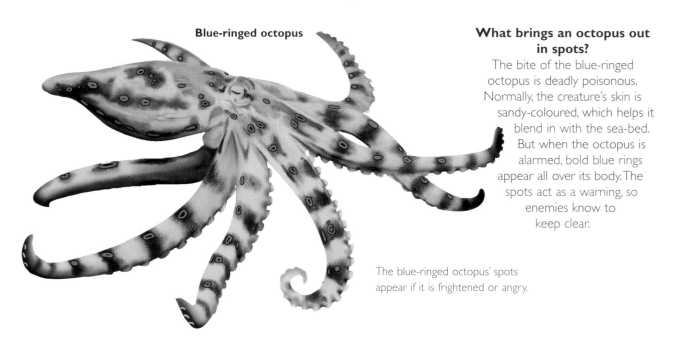

Blue-ringed octopus

What brings an octopus out in spots?

The bite of the blue-ringed octopus is deadly poisonous. Normally, the creature's skin is sandy-coloured, which helps it blend in with the sea-bed. But when the octopus is alarmed, bold blue rings appear all over its body. The spots act as a warning, so enemies know to keep clear.

The blue-ringed octopus' spots appear if it is frightened or angry.

How does a jellyfish sting?

The long, trailing tentacles of jellyfish are armed with thousands of tiny stinging cells. Some cells contain tightly-coiled barbs. When a careless fish brushes against a tentacle, the barbs fire to pierce the victim's skin and release a paralyzing poison.

Lionfish

Which is the world's most poisonous reptile?

The bite of the yellow-bellied sea snake is 50 times more powerful than that of the dreaded king cobra. Its bold yellow-and-black colours warn of danger.

Why are lionfish brightly striped?

The lionfish is a beautiful but deadly fish of tropical waters. Its long, graceful spines contain a lethal poison. The lionfish drifts lazily though the water with its orange-striped colouring, yet few enemies dare to approach it. The fish's bright colours warn that it is poisonous. They are a signal known and recognized throughout the animal world.

What "stone" can kill you if you tread on it?

Sea wasp

OVER 50 DIFFERENT KINDS OF POISONOUS FISH LURK IN THE WORLD'S OCEANS. Some are armed with venomous spines, others have poisonous flesh. The stonefish of Australian waters is one of the deadliest of all sea creatures. If a person treads on the fish, its spines release a toxin (poison) that causes agonizing pain. Numbness spreads through the victim's body, and they may die of shock, heart failure or breathing problems.

In Australian waters, the scary sea wasp jellyfish is responsible for more deaths than sharks.

The lionfish's striped colours warn enemies to keep well away.

What sea creature can sting a person to death in four minutes?

Jellyfish look fragile, but many species are armed with painful stings. The box jellyfish of South-east Asia is so venomous that its sting can kill a person in just four minutes. The small sea wasp jellyfish of Australia is said to have the world's most painful sting.

Which deadly fish looks like a toad?

The toadfish is a poisonous fish that dwells on the sea-bed in warm oceans. The spines on its back fins and gill covers contain a strong venom that can cause great pain. With its bulging eyes, large mouth and blotchy skin, the fish is well-named, for it looks just like a toad.

Which poisonous fish do people eat?

The entrails of the pufferfish contain a powerful poison. Yet other parts of the fish are said to taste delicious! In Japan, the fish is served as a delicacy called fugu. Japanese chefs are trained to remove all traces of the poisonous organs, yet each year people die from eating fugu that has not been properly prepared.

What is the stingray's secret weapon?

Stingrays live and hunt on the ocean bottom. Their long, thin tails are armed with barbs that can inject a painful poison.

Which marine reptile is the biggest?

The saltwater crocodile is the world's largest sea-going reptile. This fierce giant grows up to 8 m (26 feet) long, and its jaws and teeth are jumbo-sized to match!

Saltwater or estuarine crocodiles are found on eastern sea coasts from India to Australia.

What sea creature is as big as four dinosaurs?

Speedy orcas grow up to 9 m (30 feet) long and weigh over 6 tonnes.

THE BLUE WHALE IS THE GIANT OF THE OCEANS. INDEED, IT IS the largest animal ever to have lived on Earth – four times the size of the biggest dinosaur! An adult blue whale measures up to 32 m (100 feet) long, and may weigh over 200 tonnes – as much as 60 elephants. Female blue whales are the biggest – the males are smaller.

What is the smallest fish?

The dwarf goby holds the record for the world's smallest fish. Adult dwarf gobies measure only 1 cm (0.4 in) long – about the width of your little finger. These tiny fish are found in the Indian Ocean.

What is the world's biggest crab?

The Japanese spider crab is the giant of the crab world. Its body measures more than 30 cm (1 ft) across, and a rowing boat would easily fit between its outstretched claws, which grow up to an astonishing span of 3.5 m (11 feet). At the other end of the scale, the tiniest crab is smaller than a pea.

What record-breaking fish came back to life?

Coelacanths are giant primitive fish that scientists knew from fossils, but believed had died out millions of years ago. Then in 1938, a living specimen of the "extinct" species was caught off South Africa. Now scientists in submersibles have studied coelacanths living on the sea-bed off the island of Madagascar. Coelacanths are giant, blue-scaled fish with muscly fins which they may use to perch on the ocean bottom.

Killer whale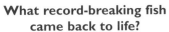

What is the world's largest mollusc?

MOLLUSCS ARE A FAMILY OF SHELLED CREATURES THAT INCLUDE SLUGS,

snails, clams, and also squid and octopus. The largest mollusc is the giant squid. These creatures commonly grow 3.6 m (12 feet) long, but specimens as large as 21 m (69 feet) have been found washed up on beaches. Scientists know little about these mysterious deep-sea creatures, which have never been seen swimming in the ocean depths.

What is the biggest fish?

Fish vary more in size than any other group of animals with backbones (vertebrates). The largest fish is the whale shark, which grows up to 15 m (49 feet) long and weighs 20 tonnes. Though giant in size, whale sharks are not fierce hunters. They feed mainly on tiny shrimp-like creatures called krill.

What are the tiniest sea creatures?

Thousands of kinds of tiny creatures live in the world's oceans. The smallest are made up of just one cell, and must be magnified a thousand times or more before we can see them. Plankton is the name given to the billions of tiny plants and animals that float near the surface of the oceans. They are the main food of many fish and other sea creatures.

Which is the fastest marine mammal?

The orca, or killer whale, is the speed champion among sea creatures. It can race along at up to 56 kph (34 mph) to overtake its prey.

What is a chimera?

According to Greek legend, the Chimera was a terrible

monster with a lion's head, a goat's body and a dragon's tail. Strange deep-sea fish called chimeras also look as if their bodies have been assembled from the parts of other creatures. They have large heads with staring eyes like bushbabies, and buck teeth like rabbits. Their bodies end in long, thin tails like rats' tails.

What is a kraken?

In olden days, myths and legends about dangerous sea creatures reflected the perils of ocean travel. Norwegian legends told of the kraken, a giant, many-armed monster that rose from the depths, wrapped its tentacles around unlucky ships and dragged them down to the bottom. This legend is thought to be based on sightings of the mysterious deep-sea squid.

What is a mermaid's purse?

Dogfish are small sharks. The tough case in which a baby dogfish develops is called a mermaid's purse. Sometimes the empty cases are found washed up on beaches, but it is unlikely that mermaids keep their treasures there!

Which fish has devil's horns?

The manta ray or devilfish has two fins that curve forward from its head like devil's horns. The ray uses its "horns" to scoop food into its mouth as it swims along the sea-bed.

Are there sea monsters in Massachusetts?

Early American settlers lived in fear of a huge sea serpent that was said to live off the coast of Gloucester, Massachusetts. The monster was supposed to have been scaly with a long tongue, but nobody really knows what it looked like – or if it even existed!

Manta ray

Which white whale ate Captain Ahab's leg?

Herman Melville's classic novel, *Moby Dick*, tell the story of Captain Ahab and his hunt for the great white sperm whale that tore off his leg. In his ship, the *Pequod*, Ahab and his sailors sail all around the world in search of the whale. When they finally catch up with Moby Dick, they struggle for three days to catch him. Ahab finally harpoons the great monster just as the whale sinks the ship, and the unfortunate captain is dragged down to a watery grave.

Which nymph ate sailors?

An ancient Greek legend tells of a beautiful nymph, called Scylla, who argued with the Gods and was turned into a terrifying monster by them. This horrific creature was said to have six heads, each with three rows of teeth. It lived in a sea cave, but would venture out of the deep to prey on creatures like dolphins, sharks and even sailors!

Who survived being eaten by a whale?

According to the Bible's Old Testament, a man called Jonah was travelling by sea when a storm blew up. Superstitious sailors cast the unlucky traveller overboard. A whale swallowed Jonah, but spat him out unharmed three days later. In reality, no one could survive in a whale's stomach for three days, because there would be no air to breathe.

The giant manta ray looks scary, but is generally harmless to humans.

What fish carries the "sword of the sea"?

The killer whale has a tall, thin back fin 2 m (6.5 feet) long, that sticks straight out of the water like a sword. Another sea creature, the swordfish, has a long snout shaped like a sword, but edged with tiny teeth. This large, powerful hunter catches its prey by swimming among a shoal of fish and slashing about wildly with its "sword". There have also been reports of swordfish piercing and sinking boats.

Do unicorns live in the sea?

Narwhals are small whales that swim in icy Arctic waters. Male narwhals have a strange left tooth that grows outwards from the gum to form a long, spiralling tusk. In times past, narwhals' tusks found on beaches were sold as precious unicorn horns.

Are mermaids real?

IN BYGONE TIMES, SAILORS WHO HAD SPENT LONG MONTHS at sea sometimes reported seeing mermaids – creatures with the head and body of a woman and a fish's tail. Experts now believe these stories may have been inspired by dugongs – rare sea mammals with rounded faces which hold their bodies upright in the water.

Female dugongs sometimes cuddle their babies in their front flippers while they suckle, another human-like trait.

Dugong

Hammerhead shark

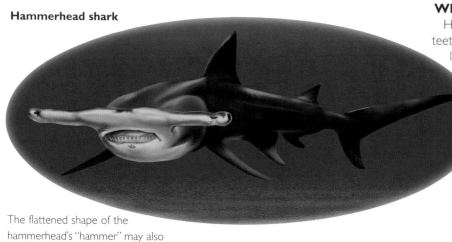

The flattened shape of the hammerhead's "hammer" may also help it float and manoeuvre.

What has up to 3,000 teeth?

Hunting sharks have triangular teeth with serrated (jagged) edges like a saw. A shark may have as many as 3,000 teeth in its mouth, arranged in up to 20 rows, but only the teeth on the outer edge of the jaw are actually used for biting. The inner teeth move outwards to replace worn or broken teeth, so the shark's working set remain razor-sharp.

Are all sharks deadly?

No. Scientists have identified about 380 different kinds of shark. Relatively few species are fierce predators that hunt large prey such as seals, squid and penguins. Most sharks, such as whale sharks and basking sharks, feed on tiny creatures which they filter from the water using their sieve-like mouths. No harm will come to you if you meet one – unless you die of fright!

Which shark has a head like a hammer?

THE HAMMERHEAD SHARK IS NAMED FOR ITS CURIOUS HEAD, SHAPED like a giant letter "T". The shark's eyes and nostrils are set on the ends of its "hammer". As it moves along the sea-bed, it swings its head from side to side. Some scientists believe that the widely spaced eyes and nostrils help the hammerhead to home in on its prey.

The great white shark is nicknamed "white death". Its scientific name means "jagged teeth".

How do sharks track down their prey?

SHARKS HAVE MANY SENSES THAT HELP WITH HUNTING. AN excellent sense of smell allows the shark to detect tiny amounts of blood dissolved in the water, and track down distant wounded animals. A special sense called "distant touch" helps it to pick up vibrations caused by swimming creatures. At closer range, sensory pores on the shark's snout detect tiny electrical signals given off by prey animals' muscles. Sight and hearing also help the shark as it moves in for the kill.

What would sink if it didn't swim?
Most fish have a special organ called a swim bladder that helps them to float. Sharks have no swim bladder, so they must keep swimming to avoid sinking. Moving forward also keeps a supply of oxygen-rich sea-water flowing over the shark's gills, which helps it breathe.

What makes one shark bite another?
The smell of blood sometimes excites sharks so much they go into a "feeding frenzy". A group of feeding sharks will start to snap wildly and bite one another, and may even tear one of their number to pieces in the excitement.

Great white shark

What is the world's most deadly shark?
The great white shark is the world's most feared sea creature. It is responsible for more attacks on humans than any other shark. Great whites grow to 7 m (23 feet) long. Their jaws are so powerful they can sever a human arm or leg in a single bite. Tiger and mako sharks are also known as killers.

What creature holds the record for long-distance ocean travel?
Grey whales are the champion travellers of the oceans. Each year, they journey from their breeding grounds in the tropics to feeding grounds in the Arctic, and back again – a round trip of up to 20,000 km (12,500 miles).

Grey whale

Grey whales swim such huge distances on migration that scientists use satellites to track them.

Can dolphins talk?
Dolphins make all sorts of noises, from clicks and squeals to groans and whistles. A school of hunting dolphins keep in constant touch with one another through these noises, and "talk" together to co-ordinate their hunt.

Each dolphin has its own special whistle which helps the other members of its school to pinpoint its position during a hunt.

Why do whales and dolphins come to the surface?

WHALES AND DOLPHINS LOOK A LOT LIKE FISH, BUT THEY ARE REALLY sea-going mammals. Like all mammals, they breathe oxygen from the air, and so must surface to breathe. One or two nostrils called blowholes on top of the animal's head allow it to breathe without lifting its head from the water. But dolphins and some whales sometimes rear right out of the water to look around, a technique called spy-hopping.

Dolphins

What hunts by sonar?

Dolphins hunt with the aid of their own built-in sonar system, called echolocation. As they swim along, they produce a stream of clicking sounds. Sound waves from the clicks spread out through the water. When they hit an object, such as a shoal of fish, they bounce back. The dolphin can sense the size and movements of its prey by listening to the echoes.

What sleeps in a duvet of seaweed?

The sea otter makes its home among the kelp weed beds of the eastern Pacific. While resting, the otter wraps seaweed fronds around its body so it does not drift away with the ocean currents.

What eats its lunch in a bubble?

Humpback whales feed on small fish and krill floating near the sea surface. Sometimes they use a technique called bubble-netting to catch their prey. The whale lurks below a shoal of fish, then swims slowly upwards, blowing a stream of bubbles. The fish are trapped inside the net of bubbles and cannot escape from the whale's open jaws.

Which is the friendliest sea creature?

Dolphins are naturally playful and friendly to humans. They often swim alongside boats, riding on the bow-wave. Dolphins called "friendlies" regularly visit tourist beaches to swim with holiday-makers. There are many reports of dolphins rescuing drowning people, and even saving swimmers from sharks.

The sea otter is a skillful tool-user

Which is the cleverest sea creature?

DOLPHINS ARE AMONG THE WORLD'S MOST intelligent creatures. Tests in aquariums show they learn to perform new tasks quickly, and can even pass on their skills by "talking" to dolphins in other tanks. Sea otters are clever too, for they are one of the few animals able to use tools. The otter feeds on sea urchins, crabs and other shelled creatures. It breaks open the shells by smashing them against a flat rock balanced on its chest.

Sea otter

Which sea creature feeds on its mate's blood?

Deep-sea anglerfish have unusual sex lives. The females are up to 20 times bigger than the males! When a tiny male meets a female, he clamps on to her side with his powerful jaws and won't let go. Eventually he becomes fused to her body and feeds on her blood. The female has a handy supply of sperm to fertilize her eggs – but has to carry the "hanger-on" wherever she goes.

Which creature has a midwife at the birth?

Pregnant dolphins give birth to a single baby up to a year after mating. Experienced female dolphins known as "midwives" help at the birth. They may support the mother's body or help lift the baby to the surface so it can breathe.

What makes a fiddler crab sexy?

Male fiddler crabs have a built-in "sex symbol" – one claw that is much bigger than the other. On the sea-shore, the males attract attention by scuttling up and down waving their giant claws. The females choose the most energetic males with the biggest claws to mate with.

How do humpback whales go courting?

Humpback whales make many different sounds, including clicks, squeaks, moans and roars. To attract a partner, the male humpback sings a "song" made up of different noises. Each male sings a different tune, lasting for hours or even days. Humans enjoy the whale-song too – recordings of humpbacks have been made into hit CDs.

How do deep-sea creatures light up each others' lives?

In the darkness of the deep sea, many fish use light to attract a mate. Deep-sea viperfish and dragonfish have lines of tiny lights running along their bellies. Males and females have different patterns of lights, and can recognize the opposite sex when they see the right pattern.

The fiddler crab's giant claw gives him sex appeal, but is little help when feeding.

Fiddler crab

How do octopuses show their feelings?

Octopus and squid can change their skin colour from brown to green or blue. They use this skill to camouflage themselves when hunting, but also change colour to express emotions such as anger, and to attract a mate.

How does the damsel fish look after its eggs?

Most fish take little care of their eggs – they just spawn (lay and fertilize their eggs) and swim away without a backward glance. Some kinds of damsel fish are different. The females glue their eggs carefully to rocks. The males are caring fathers. They guard and check the eggs until they hatch, and shoo off any other fish that approach to eat them.

Which male fish gets pregnant?

Sea-horses have extraordinary breeding habits. The female lays her eggs in a little pouch on the male sea-horse's belly. The eggs develop in the safety of the pouch. About a month later, an amazing sight occurs, as the male "gives birth" to hundreds of tiny sea-horses.

Green turtles

Green turtles swim hundreds of kilometres to lay their eggs on the beach where they hatched out.

What sea creature comes ashore to breed?

GREEN TURTLES SPEND THEIR WHOLE LIVES AT SEA, but come on land to breed. The female swims ashore and clambers up the beach. Then she digs a deep hole and lays her eggs. When the baby turtles hatch they dig themselves out of the sand, then dash down to the waves and swim away quickly.

Blue whales

A blue whale calf drinks 100 litres (175 pints) of its mother's milk a day.

Which creature has the world's largest baby?

FEMALE BLUE WHALES, THE LARGEST WHALES, ALSO BEAR THE biggest babies. A newborn blue whale calf measures 7 m (23 feet) long and may weigh 2.5 tonnes – as much as a full-grown elephant! The thirsty baby drinks huge quantities of its mother's milk and puts on weight fast. At six months old, it may be as much as 16 m (54 feet) long.

What glues its eggs to the roof of its cave?

Female octopuses breed only once in their lifetime. After mating, the female lays long strings of eggs and glues them to the roof of her cave. She tends her eggs for up to six weeks, and never leaves her lair to go hunting. Many females die of hunger or exhaustion before their eggs hatch out.

What fish swims a long way to breed?

Young salmon hatch out and grow in shallow streams inland. After several years, they swim downriver to the sea and spend their adult lives in the ocean. To breed, they swim back and fight their way upriver, to spawn in the same stream where they hatched out.

What creature's birth was a mystery for centuries?

Eels were once a common sight in European streams and rivers. But their breeding habits were a mystery, for the eggs and baby eels were never seen. Then in the 1920s, experts at last discovered that the eels swim downriver and make their way across the Atlantic to breed. They spawn in the warm waters of the Sargasso Sea off the coast of Florida. When the eggs hatch out, the young eels drift slowly back to Europe and swim upriver.

How do young sea otters learn their skills?

Otters are naturally playful creatures. Young sea otters chase each other through the waving seaweeds and turn somersaults in the water. Mother otters sometimes bring their young an injured fish to play with. As the pups take turns to catch their weakened prey, they learn hunting skills that will be vital when they are older.

Sea catfish

Which young fish eats its brothers and sisters?

Sand tiger shark eggs hatch out inside their mother's body. The tiny embryo sharks feed on one another until only one big, strong baby is left, ready to be born.

How does the dugong protect its baby?

Female dugongs give birth to a single calf a year after mating. A close bond forms between mother and baby. As the female and her calf swim through the murky sea-grass, she calls out constantly, to make sure her baby is safe.

Which sea father has a mouthful of babies?

FEW FISH LOOK AFTER THEIR BABIES, BUT FISH known as mouthbrooders are the exception. Mouthbrooders such as sea catfish protect their young by hiding them in their mouths! In sea catfish, the male is the caring parent. The babies swim in a cloud near their dad's head. When danger threatens they scoot back inside his mouth.

Young catfish swim close to their father's mouth so they can dash inside if danger approaches.

Index

Corrective Reading

▶Concept Applications

Comprehension C
Teachers Guide

Siegfried Engelmann • Susan Hanner • Phyllis Haddox

SRA
McGraw-Hill

Columbus, Ohio

A Division of The McGraw-Hill Companies

PHOTO CREDITS
Cover Photo: KS Studios

SRA/McGraw-Hill
*A Division of The **McGraw·Hill** Companies*

2002 Imprint
Copyright © 1999 by SRA/McGraw-Hill.

Send all inquiries to:
SRA/McGraw-Hill
8787 Orion Place
Columbus, OH 43240-4027

Printed in the United States of America.

ISBN 0-02-674817-7

6 7 8 9 DBH 04

Contents

Contents

SRA's Corrective Reading Series:

SRA's *Corrective Reading* programs are divided into two strands: Decoding and Comprehension.

A single-strand sequence places students in one strand (**Comprehension**, for example), and the students move through the strand from the point of initial placement (**Comprehension A, B1, B2,** or **C**) to the end of the strand (**Comprehension C**).

The double-strand sequence requires that students receive two full periods of instruction each day—one period in a Decoding program and one period in a Comprehension program.

Each **Comprehension** program is designed to be used independently. Students may be placed at the beginning of one program and complete all the lessons in that program in either a single-strand or double-strand sequence.

Comprehension Strand: A, B1, B2, C

The development of skills through the Comprehension programs proceeds from separate component skills to applications that integrate the skills. The programs also progress from comprehending oral language to comprehending written material. Skills are first taught in a highly structured form that is tightly controlled by the teacher. Eventually, students are shown how to apply the skills independently to complex written materials.

Here is a diagram of the four Comprehension programs in SRA's *Corrective Reading* series.

Comprehension A	Comprehension B1	Comprehension B2	Comprehension C
65 Lessons	60 Lessons	65 Lessons	140 Lessons

Students who place in **Comprehension A** do not understand the concepts underlying much of the material being taught in classrooms. They do not have well-developed recitation skills. They cannot repeat sentences they hear, so they have trouble retaining and answering questions about information that is presented. These students are often prevented from comprehending what they read because they don't even understand the material when it is presented orally.

Students who place in **Comprehension B1** exhibit many of the deficiencies observed in students who place in Level A. They lack some common basic information, such as how many months are in a year. They are deficient in thinking operations, but usually, they are more advanced in thinking operations than Level A students. Typically, they make about 15 errors on the Comprehension Placement Test. They tend to miss the difficult statement-repetition items and some of the information items. They have some trouble identifying how things are the same, and they have trouble with deductions that involve *maybe*.

Students who place in **Comprehension C** have already learned many skills. Their primary deficiency is in using those skills independently, more than it is in learning new skills. They can deduce, make inferences, and respond to specific instructions. However, they do not yet have a facility for working independently.

A COMPREHENSION PLACEMENT TEST IS AVAILABLE FOR DETERMINING THE APPROPRIATE PLACEMENT OF STUDENTS.

A reproducible copy of the *Corrective Reading* Comprehension Placement Test and details on how to administer it appear in Appendix A at the end of this guide.

The test consists of two parts. Part I, an oral test that is individually administered, provides an evaluation of these skills:

◆ recitation behavior (repeating orally presented sentences)

◆ deductions (drawing conclusions)

◆ analogies

◆ basic information (common facts that are assumed of nearly every student)

◆ divergent reasoning skills (stating how things are the same and how they are different)

Part II, a written test that can be administered to groups as well as to individual students, tests these skills:

◆ statement-inference skills (determining which word in a sentence is being defined and which words define it)

◆ rule-application skills

◆ vocabulary skills

Progress Through the Comprehension Strand

The Comprehension programs are designed so that there is a careful progression of skill development from level to level. The Comprehension strand has three entry points:

1 Students who begin at Level A should complete Levels A and B1 in a school year.

2 Students who begin at Level B1 should complete Levels B1 and B2 in a school year.

3 Students who begin at Level C should complete Level C and additional outside reading in a school year.

Features of All Comprehension Levels

Each level of SRA's *Corrective Reading* Comprehension programs have features that have been demonstrated through research studies to be effective in improving student performance.

◆ Each level is a core program, not ancillary material. Each level contains all the material you need and provides students with all the practice they need to learn the skills.

◆ All words, skills, and strategies are taught through DIRECT INSTRUCTION. This approach is the most efficient for communicating with the students, for evaluating their performance on a moment-to-moment basis, and for achieving student mastery. Students are not simply exposed to skills. Skills are taught.

◆ Students are taught everything that is required for what they are to do later. Conversely, they are not taught skills that are not needed for later skill applications. The levels concentrate only on the necessary skills, not the nuances.

◆ Each level is based on cumulative skill development. Skills and strategies are taught, with lots of examples. Once a skill or strategy is taught, students receive practice in applying that skill until the end of the level. This type of cumulative development has been demonstrated by research studies to be the most effective method for teaching skills so they become well-learned or automatic.

◆ Because of the cumulative development of skills, the difficulty of material increases gradually but steadily.

◆ Each level is divided into daily lessons that can usually be presented in a class period (35–45 minutes of teacher-directed work and independent student applications).

◆ Each level contains in-program Mastery Tests. These tests are criterion-referenced performance measures that are part of the lessons. They provide you with very detailed data on student performance. They also show the students how their performance is improving as they progress through the program.

◆ Each level includes an effective management system. Students earn points for performance on each part of the daily lesson. Records of this performance may be used for awarding grades and documenting progress in specific skill areas.

◆ Each lesson specifies both teacher and student behavior. The lessons are scripted. The scripts specify what you do and say, as well as appropriate student responses. The scripted lessons assure that you will (a) use uniform wording, (b) present examples in a manner that communicates effectively with students, and (c) be able to complete a lesson during a class period. **Note:** Research has disclosed that teachers are more effective when they follow scripted lessons.

Facts About Problem Readers

The series is designed to change the behavior of problem readers. The specific tendencies of problem readers suggest what a program must do to be effective in changing these students' behavior.

Because students who are lacking in comprehension skills are often poor decoders, they typically do not follow instructions precisely. They have often been reinforced for raising their hand and asking the teacher questions. This strategy has served them in content areas, such as science and social studies, as well as reading. As a result, they have not developed precision in following instructions that are presented orally or in writing.

Because of the way material they have studied has been sequenced, poor comprehenders also have a poor memory for information. Typically, they have never been required to learn information one day and then use it that day and from then on. The usual pattern has been for them to work with vocabulary or facts for only a lesson or two, after which the material disappears. The result is a very poorly developed strategy for remembering information, particularly systems of information that contain related facts and rules.

Poor comprehenders also have poor statement-repetition skills (primarily because they have never practiced these skills). For instance, when they are told to repeat the statement "Some of the people who live in America are illiterate," the students may say, "Some people who live in America are ill," or some other inaccurate production. The lack of statement-repetition skills places these students at a great disadvantage when they try to read and retain information, even if they decode it correctly.

Often, poor comprehenders will vascillate from being very guarded in believing what others tell them, to being very gullible, because they often lack the analytical skills required to process arguments. They often have very strong feelings and prejudices, but they are unable to articulate the evidence that supports their beliefs or the conclusions that derive from the evidence. They are not practiced with flaws in arguments that present false analogies, improper deductions, or appeals that are inappropriate (such as arguing about a whole group from information about an individual).

Poor comprehenders have a deficiency in vocabulary and common information. This deficit pre-empts them from constructing the appropriate schemata when reading about situations that assume basic information or vocabulary. They may understand the meaning of the word *colonial,* for instance, but not know the relationship of that word to *colony.*

Finally, poor comprehenders are not highly motivated students. For these students, reading has been punishing. The students often profess indifference: "I don't care if I learn that or not." But the students' behavior gives strong suggestions that they care a great deal. When they learn to use new words such as *regulate* and *participate,* they feel very proud.

The students' ineffective reading strategies and negative attitudes about reading become more ingrained as the students get older. To overcome them requires a very careful program, one that systematically replaces these strategies with new ones and that provides lots and lots of practice.

In summary, the knowledge and skills of poor comprehenders are spotty. While often exhibiting intelligent behaviors in dealing with their peers, they are remarkably naive in dealing with academic content because they don't know exactly what to attend to, precisely what it means, how to organize it, how to relate it to other known facts and remember it, how to apply it to unique situations, and how to evaluate it in terms of consistency with other facts and rules.

The Solutions

The problems of poor comprehenders suggest these solutions:

The *Corrective Reading* Comprehension programs are designed to provide extensive practice in following directions. The various activities presented in the series are designed so that students must attend to the instructions. In one lesson, for instance, the directions for an activity might be "Circle the verbs." In the next lesson, instructions for the same activity might be "Make a box around the verbs." The direct-instruction activities that address following instructions present directions that the students cannot figure out from either the format of the activity or the context. Students, therefore, learn the strategy of reading carefully and attending to the **details** of the instructions. Also, students practice writing instructions so that they develop an appreciation of what information is needed to clearly convey the operation they are trying to describe.

The series provides daily practice in statement repetition in Comprehension Levels A, B1, and B2. This practice is presented in Level A through tasks that don't involve reading. In later levels of the series, the statement-repetition activities are related increasingly to statements the students read. The emphasis on statement repetition both makes students much more facile in repeating statements (requiring only one or two attempts, compared to the many attempts that would be required early in the program) and helps reinforce the general strategy that one must be very precise when dealing with statements in what is read as well as in what is heard.

The *Corrective Reading* series is designed so that whatever is taught is used. In the Comprehension series, nothing goes away. The vocabulary that is introduced is integrated so that the students use the vocabulary in following instructions, making analogies and deductions, identifying flaws in arguments, and in various other activities. Similarly, facts that are learned are integrated and applied to a wide range of applications. This nonspiral approach to instruction demonstrates to students that they must develop strategies for retaining the information that is taught and relating it to other information. The format assures that students will be able to learn, organize, and process what is taught. Mastery Tests within the series document to both teacher and students that the skills and information presented in the program are mastered.

The Comprehension series presents various analytical skills that can be applied to higher-order thinking tasks. In fact, the *Corrective Reading* Comprehension series is possibly the only readily available source of instruction for teaching students how analogies work, how logical reasoning is applied to arguments, how conclusions depend on evidence, and how to evaluate the adequacy of the evidence. Deductions are emphasized because basic arguments that affect everyday life are usually presented as deductions. The series presents specific common fallacies (arguing from part to whole, arguing from whole to part, arguing from a false cause, arguing from limited choices). Students also learn to identify contradictions, at first simple ones, and later, those that are inferred from facts the students have learned. The focus of the series, in other words, is not simply on narrowly defined logical-reasoning skills, but on logical-reasoning skills as they apply to all aspects of reading.

To compensate for the deficiencies in vocabulary and common information, the series introduces both "fact systems" and vocabulary words. The fact systems that have been selected include: body systems (skeletal, muscular, circulatory, etc.), calendar information, animal information (classifications such as fish, amphibian, reptile, mammal, bird), economics rules (supply-demand), and plants. These systems provide a vehicle for teaching some vocabulary. Additional vocabulary is introduced in all levels. In Levels B1 and B2, vocabulary is introduced in connection with parts of speech. Some of these words were selected because they have a verb, noun, and adjective form (for example, *protect, protection,* and *protective*). In Level C, students are taught how to infer the meaning of words from context. Note that all words, once introduced, appear in various activities—from following instructions to identifying contradictions.

Finally, the series addresses the problem reader's poor self-image. The series is designed so the students can succeed in learning sophisticated skills (such as identifying the missing premise in an argument). Furthermore, a point system that is based on realistic performance goals assures that the student who tries will succeed and will receive reinforcement for improved performance.

In summary, the series uses a two-pronged approach. Each level teaches specific skills to replace the student's ineffective approach to comprehension. Each level also contains an effective management system that turns students on to reading. The approach WORKS.

The Program—Comprehension C Concept Applications

The fourth level of the Comprehension programs in SRA's *Corrective Reading* series is **Comprehension C.**

The program is made up of 140 regular lessons (numbered consecutively from 1 through 140) and 9 Fact Game and Mastery Test lessons (numbered consecutively from 1 through 9). The Fact Game and Mastery Test lessons are scheduled every fifteenth regular lesson (after Lessons 15, 30, 45, and so on).

Each lesson is designed to provide activities for a 40- to 45–minute period.

Who It's For

Comprehension C is designed for students who have completed **Comprehension B2** in the *Corrective Reading* series, and for students whose scores on the Comprehension Placement Test qualify them for entry into the program. These students are probably in grades 6 through 12, and they may even be found in junior college. The Decoding Placement Test criteria usually indicate that these students decode well enough to qualify for **Decoding C,** which is the most advanced Decoding program in the *Corrective Reading* series.

These students are also fairly proficient in comprehension skills. Specifically, they understand basic logical operations; they can draw conclusions from evidence; their basic vocabularies are reasonably broad; and their recitation and statement repetition skills are fairly good.

Students who place in **Comprehension C** have several common skill deficiencies.

◆ Although students are fairly proficient in logical reasoning, they have not mastered reasoning skills to the point where applying them is nearly automatic.

◆ They have trouble learning a new concept or discrimination from written instructions, although the same concept or discrimination would not be difficult to learn if it were presented orally by the teacher.

◆ They are deficient in advanced vocabulary.

◆ They are weak in the mechanics of writing and editing.

◆ They lack facility in extracting information from sources—such as from a written passage or a graph.

Because students are weak in foundation skills, these students should be firmed on these skills. Students also need new information about their world and about the words used to describe it. And they need sharpened skills for using the information that they have acquired.

The program may also be used developmentally for students of average or above-average ability in grades 5 through 12. Performance on the placement test indicates whether a particular student places in the program.

What Is Taught

The skills taught in **Comprehension C** fall into five categories. Three categories teach component skills and are classified as

Basic Tools. The two remaining categories teach the application of the component skills to higher-order operations and are classified Higher-Order Skills.

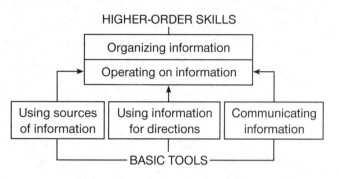

HIGHER-ORDER SKILLS

The categories are the basis on which the activities in the program are organized.

The Scope and Sequence Chart below and in Appendix B of this guide shows the specific skill areas included in each category.

The skills taught in Basic Tools are needed to perform the higher-order operations. For example, students learn to infer meaning from context, which is a basic tool. Then this skill is used to analyze arguments, a higher-order skill. Students learn to use specific reference material—a skill that is a basic tool. Then they learn the higher-order skill of how to operate on the information they find—how to determine whether it contains contradictory statements, how to organize it into outline form, and how to combine it with information from another source, such as a map or a passage.

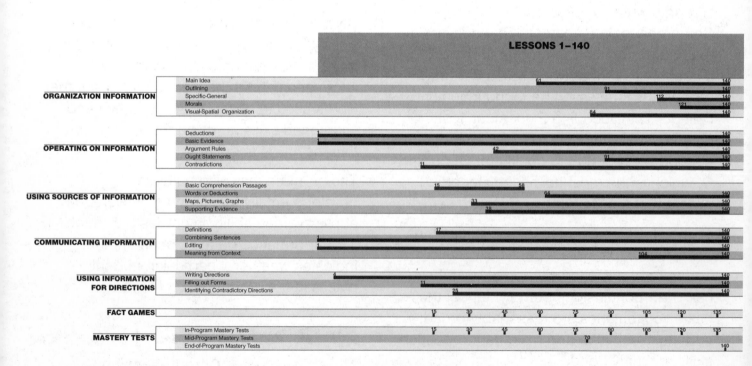

Basic Tool: Using Sources of Information

This category teaches students how to use different sources of information—passages, graphs, maps, and illustrations. Students first learn conventions and procedures for decoding a map or an illustration. They then engage in activities that require the use of two sources, for example, a map and a passage, a passage and an illustration, or two passages. Students use the sources to answer questions, and they also indicate which source answers a particular question. In one variation of this activity, two passages are presented that contradict each other on major points. Students learn that they must use a third, reliable reference source such as a dictionary or an encyclopedia to find evidence that resolves the contradiction.

These skills reinforce the students' ability to make deductions and to organize information.

Basic Tool: Using Information for Directions

The focus of this category is on precise use of language. Students practice this skill in three major activities. In one activity, they use information about fictitious people to fill out forms, such as loan applications or rental agreements. In another, simple diagrams are presented, and students are instructed to write the directions for creating the diagram. In yet another activity, they are presented with a diagram and a set of directions for drawing the diagram. Part of the directions contradict certain details in the diagram. Students identify the contradictory part and draw a diagram that is consistent with the directions.

Basic Tool: Communicating Information

When students are deficient in vocabulary and lack basic skills in written communication, they may be unable to convey information. This category has two objectives—to introduce new vocabulary and to teach specific skills that are essential to written communication.

Vocabulary is introduced in several kinds of activities. Perhaps the most important instruction provided for this skill is the presentation of new vocabulary through model sentences. Students first memorize a model sentence, such as **By** <u>hesitating,</u> **she lost her** <u>opportunity.</u> Students learn the meaning of the underlined words, and then they use the new words in other writing and editing exercises. In another type of activity, students must infer the meaning of a new word from the context of the passage in which it appears. New vocabulary is also introduced in a dictionary-type format. Every ten lessons, beginning in Lesson 70, about five new words are presented. For each word, there is a simple definition and a sentence using the word.

To improve written communication, students learn rules for combining sentences with words such as **who, which, however,** and **therefore.** Students also edit passages, concentrating on redundant information and subject-verb agreement.

Higher-Order Skill: Organizing Information

The skills taught in this category include identifying the main idea, outlining, making statements either more general or more specific than original statements, generalizing from specific events to come up with a moral, and expressing information in visual-spatial displays. All of these skills are closely related to the skills taught in Using Sources of Information.

Higher-Order Skill: Operating on Information

After information has been found and organized, it can be operated on. Specific operations taught include using evidence, drawing conclusions, making up arguments, and analyzing the validity of arguments. There is particular emphasis on faulty arguments and propaganda. Students learn rules about faulty arguments, such as **Just because two things happen around the same time doesn't mean one thing causes the other thing.** Students also learn to judge whether sources of information are reliable. The analysis of faulty arguments is applied to advertisements and other biased appeals similar to those that reach the students in everyday life.

Assessing Student Performance and Meeting Behavioral Objectives

The various skills outlined in the preceding section are presented frequently enough to ensure mastery. Once a skill is taught in one category, it is reviewed and integrated with activities from other categories.

To permit you to assess student performance and to indicate the specific behavioral objectives that have been achieved by the students, criterion-referenced tests are included in the program itself as part of the instructional sequence.

The tests cover factual information, vocabulary, and optional writing-rate activities.

In-Program Tests

Comprehension C has a thorough criterion-referenced testing schedule for the skills taught in the program. Included in the tests are: tests on information (which start at Lesson 20 and occur every fifth lesson early in the program and assume a more irregular schedule); vocabulary tests (which start at Lesson 25 and occur every fifth lesson); independent lessons (which start at Lesson 50 and occur every tenth lesson); and the in-program Mastery Tests (which follow the Fact Games). On the following page is a chart that summarizes the in-program tests.

The program provides an optional activity daily for those students whose writing rate is unacceptably slow. The students must copy a short passage within a specified amount of time. The criterion rate at the beginning of the program is 28 to 30 words per 2 minutes. By the end of the program, the criterion is 40 to 46 words per two minutes.

If students do the writing-rate activities, they should record their progress on the Writing Rate Progress Charts at the back of the Workbook. For each lesson, students enter the number of words copied correctly for the 2-minute period. If students have trouble filling in the graph, help them. Explain that every five lessons, they should connect the dots and see the progress they have made.

	FG/MT 1	20	25	30	FG/MT 2	35	40	45	FG/MT 3	50	55	60
Information Test		✔	✔	✔		✔	✔			✔	✔	✔
Vocabulary Test			✔	✔		✔	✔	✔		✔	✔	✔
Independent Lesson											✔	✔
Mastery Test	✔				✔				✔			

	FG/MT 4	65	70	75	FG/MT 5	80	85	90	FG/MT 6	95	100	105
Information Test			✔				✔				✔	
Vocabulary Test		✔	✔	✔		✔	✔	✔		✔	✔	✔
Independent Lesson			✔			✔		✔			✔	
Mastery Test	✔				✔				✔			

	FG/MT 7	110	115	120	FG/MT 8	125	130	135	FG/MT 9	140
Information Test		✔		✔			✔			✔
Vocabulary Test		✔	✔	✔		✔	✔	✔		✔
Independent Lesson		✔		✔			✔			✔
Mastery Test	✔				✔				✔	

The Materials

The materials for **Comprehension C** consist of this Teacher's Guide, two Teacher Presentation Books, the Student Book, the Workbook, and mid-program and end-of-program Mastery Tests.

This Teacher's Guide contains basic information about the program and specific directions for presenting exercises and for correcting mistakes.

The Teacher Presentation Books provide a script for each lesson. Scripts specify what the teacher and the students are to say and do during a lesson.

There is a standard pattern for skill introduction in **Comprehension C.** A new skill is generally introduced first in the Student Book. The student reads an explanation of the new concept or skill, and the teacher directs the student's use of the skill. After the skill has been practiced in a few lessons, it appears in the Workbook, where it becomes an independent skill. Although students read the teaching presentation in the Student Book, the teacher structures the reading and presents tasks that supplement those that appear in the student material.

Scheduling

Here are some general considerations for scheduling students for the program.

◆ A lesson should be presented every day at an assigned time.

◆ The lesson will take about 45 minutes, depending on the size of the group. Most of the period, however, is spent on independent work.

Placement Procedures

Students are placed in **Comprehension C** based on their performance on the **Corrective Reading** Comprehension Placement Test. Details on how to administer the test appear in Appendix A of this guide.

The Lessons

Regular Lessons (1–140)

An average regular lesson contains six to eight activities and lasts approximately 45 minutes. Usually, the first two to four activities in a lesson are structured, or teacher directed. The remaining activities are independent. Finally, there is the Workcheck, during which students exchange books and papers, then mark and correct errors.

During the first ten lessons, all activities are presented in the Workbook. Lessons 11 through 140 require both the Student Book and Workbook. Typically, structured activities are presented in the Student Book and are the first exercises in the lesson. Independent activities appear in the Workbook and are completed after the Student Book activities. There are also some independent activities in the Student Book.

Fact Game and Mastery Test Lessons

Nine lessons that review and test key information and skills are presented on a regular schedule throughout **Comprehension C.** After every fifteenth lesson is a Fact Game and Mastery Test lesson. These lessons are designed for a full period and should be scheduled on the period following completion of Lessons 15, 30, 45, and so on.

Awarding Points

A point system motivates the students to perform well. It also facilitates grading. The fundamental rule about points is that all points are awarded for good performance. The students must know the rules for earning points, and they must work for every point earned.

By awarding points for good performance, you give the students a reason for working. You also provide them with a demonstration of their growing competence.

The students may earn as many as 15 points for each regular lesson. The students receive points **only for written work** on these lessons. The point schedule below is used throughout the program.

0 errors—15 points
1-2 errors—12 points
3-5 errors— 8 points
6-9 errors— 5 points
more than 9 errors— 0 points

In lessons that contain information and vocabulary tests, the students may earn 5 bonus points for no errors on the test. The students also earn points for other written work completed on test days.

For Fact Game and Mastery Test lessons, students earn points for performance on the Fact Game, and points for Mastery Test performance. Here is a schedule of points.

Fact Game: 1 point for each correct answer; 5 bonus points for earning a specified number of points.

Mastery Test: 1 point for each correct answer; 5 bonus points for a perfect score on the Mastery Test.

Recording Points

The students record their points in their Workbooks, filling in the boxes that appear next to the lesson number for that day. For each regular lesson, they enter their Workbook and Student Book points in the box marked **W,** their bonus points in the box marked **B,** and their total points in the box marked **T.**

After every fifteenth lesson is a Fact Game and Mastery Test lesson. For these lessons, students enter their Fact Game points in the box marked **FG,** their Mastery Test points in the box marked **MT,** their bonus points in the box marked **Bonus,** and their total points in the box marked **T.**

The students then record their total points for each lesson on the Point Summary Chart, which is on the inside front cover of the Workbook. Every 16 lessons, they total their points.

Bonus Points

If a student shows unusual effort or does a particularly good job, award bonus points. It is recommended, however, that no more than 2 or 3 bonus points be awarded to any student on a regular lesson day.

Confirming Points

After the students record their points, confirm their totals by checking to see that all mistakes (marked with X's) have been corrected. Then record the total on the Teacher's Record Chart. (A reproducible chart appears in Appendix F.) The students must correct their mistakes before you record points on your chart.

Below is a sample of a Teacher's Record Chart filled in for block 5, Lesson 61 through Fact Game/Mastery Test 5.

RECORD SUMMARY CHART

Student's Name	LESSON 61	62	63	64	65	66	67	68	69	70	71	72	73	74	75	FG/MT5
Thomas Quentin	15	15	15	15	20	15	15	15	15	25	15	15	15	15	25	16
Lily Sanchez	12	15	12	12	15	12	8	5	8	20	12	15	12	8	15	8

The schedule below is recommended for determining letter grades.

> A—average of 12 points or more
>   per lesson for a grading period
> B—average of 8–11 points
> C—average of 5–7 points
> D—average of less than 5 points

Those students who are properly placed in the program but who fail to earn an A or a B either lack motivation or are being taught improperly. The procedures in the next section help shape your presentation so that it is clear and helps to reinforce what the lesson is teaching.

Teaching Effectively

The most difficult management skills are those associated with presenting the various activities. To be effective, you should be businesslike, keep up a fast pace, and be responsive. Convey the impression that the material is important and interesting and that the students can achieve if they work hard. This orientation is extremely important. If you present a strong model, the students will respond in predictable and desirable ways.

Setup for the Lesson

Assign permanent seating. Seating should be arranged so that you can have eye contact with every student. There should be enough space for you to walk behind the students and monitor their work. Lower-performing students should be seated where they can be monitored quickly and frequently.

Establish procedures for distributing Student Books, Workbooks, lined paper, and sharpened pencils to the students at the beginning of the period, and for returning the materials to a specified place at the end of the period. Lesson time should not be lost while the students sharpen pencils, get Workbooks, or prepare to work with the material. When the period begins, every student should be seated, with the necessary material in place.

Pacing

Proper pacing is essential for your presentation to be effective. To ensure smooth pacing during the structured segment of each lesson:

◆ Familiarize yourself with the exercises that you are to present. Rehearse them aloud if necessary. Make sure that you can present them without having to continually look at the material.

◆ Present the material so that you set the pace. It is your responsibility to change the students' behavior. Do not permit them to shape your behavior by having you constantly repeat tasks or respond to irrelevant questions. Say your lines quickly. Correct mistakes immediately. Answer any reasonable questions, but do not permit students to interrupt during a task. Set time limits for tasks that tend to drag. Praise students who perform within time constraints.

Note: If you respond to student attempts to pull you off task, some students may learn more about pulling you off task than they will about the program skills.

Monitoring Student Behavior

Walk among the students as you present structured tasks. You do not have to stand in front of the group. Very few activities require you to write on the chalkboard or point to things that the students are to observe. Nearly all tasks require listening, reading, or both. These can be presented from any place in the room.

Structured Activities

When the students write responses to teacher-directed activities, try to check all the lower performers' work by the time they complete an exercise. To do this, spend at least half your time observing what the lower performers write and the remaining time seeing what the other students write.

Independent Activities

If you observe a tendency for some students to miss particular kinds of items, stop the students and call attention to the item. Say

Be careful with item 12. Remember the difference between the part of a group and the whole group. Do **not** tell the students the answer to any independent item, because their point total is based on their work. If you give answers, the record of their performance becomes unreliable. However, you may warn them about problem items.

As you monitor, provide the students with feedback. Tell them if an item is wrong. Say That's wrong. Try again. Mark the item with an X. Use a distinctive colored pencil—blue, orange, etc. The item will be marked as an error for the point total; however, the student receives feedback. You can tell the student the correct answer to the item if necessary, but just make sure that the item is marked as an error and that other students don't hear the correct answer.

Also, comment on good performance. Say Nearly everybody is getting the items in part B correct. I'm really pleased. These comments, as the students write, should not be so frequent that they prevent the students from concentrating. They should be frequent enough, however, to show the students that you are looking at what they do and that you are responding to it.

Workcheck

Schedule 10 to 15 minutes at the end of the period for a Workcheck. What the Workcheck includes is specified in the teacher directions for each lesson. The Workcheck **is not merely paper grading.** The idea is to let the students see their mistakes, to give them the correct answers, and to have them correct each missed item. If possible, they should make these changes before the period is completed. It may be more practical to check the students' work from the previous day at the beginning of a period. This variation is perfectly acceptable, so long as the basic order of events is maintained. The Workcheck for a lesson should be done before the students begin the next lesson.

The Workcheck procedure, starting with Lesson 3 in the Workbook and Lesson 11 in the Student Book, involves these steps:

1 The students exchange their Workbooks and Student Book papers after they complete their independent work.

2 For each independent Workbook activity, call on the students to read the **item and answer.** For Student Book activities, you read each item and call on a student for the answer.

3 The students mark an X next to every item that is incorrect.

4 The students total the number of errors, determine the points earned, and enter the total at the top of the Workbook page.

5 Workbooks and papers are returned, and each student then corrects every error.

6 Each student shows you (or your aide) that each item marked with an X has been corrected. To show that the work has been corrected, you can either initial the page, circle the point total, or use some other symbol to verify that the points have been earned. Without verification that all items have been corrected, the students earn no points for the lesson.

General Information

How Material Is Introduced

New skills are introduced in material that the students read. At specified points in the material, you ask questions. These points are indicated on the reproduced student page by circled capital letters. These letters correspond to the circled letters in the teacher's material. On the following page is an example of an exercise that introduces a new skill. The material at the top is taken from the Student Book. The material below it is from the corresponding teacher presentation.

Format Style

A format is an exercise set up in a specific form. Here are some conventions that are used in the formats for this program.

Heading

The task heading in the teacher presentation indicates the number of the exercise and the skill being taught. In the example just discussed, analyzing arguments is the skill taught in Exercise 2.

Typography

◆ This blue type indicates what you say.

◆ **This bold, blue type indicates a word or phrase that you should stress.**

◆ (This type indicates what you do.)

◆ *This type indicates the students' response.*

Numbering

Every exercise in the teacher presentation is divided into numbered steps. Numbering makes the format easier to read and provides you with some reference points. Numbering also helps you pace the presentation. Pause briefly before beginning a new step.

B

Here s a new rule:

> **Just because two things happen around the same time doesn t mean that one thing causes the other thing.**

Read the rule over to yourself and get ready to say it. (D)

The argument below is faulty because it breaks the rule.
Read the argument.

> **I went to Chicago, and it rained in Chicago. I went to Cleveland, and it rained in Cleveland. So I think I ll go to New York City and make it rain there.**

What does the writer want us to conclude? (E)
Why does the writer think that going to a city causes rain? (F)
Say the rule the argument breaks. (G)

Here s how you could prove that going to a city could not cause rain. Send the person to lots of cities. If it doesn t rain **every time** the person goes to one of those cities, going to the city does not cause rain.

═══ EXERCISE 2 ═══

ANALYZING ARGUMENTS

1. (Have the students find part B.)
2. (Call on individual students to read part B.)
   - (D) Do it. (Wait. Call on individual students to say the rule.)
   - (E) (Call on a student.) Idea: By going to any city, the writer can make it rain there.
   - (F) (Call on a student.) Idea: Because it rained in several cities while the writer was there.
   - (G) Say it. *Just because two things happen around the same time doesn't mean that one thing causes the other thing.*

Student Responses

When the format requires the students to answer a question, the response is always specified. When the format requires the students to repeat a statement, no student response is specified, because the response is the same as the statement.

If a question has more than one possible answer, the students' response is preceded by the phrase: "Accept reasonable responses, such as . . ."

The responses for some items begin with the word "Idea." For these items, various wordings are appropriate. The sample responses provided in the teacher's material are samples, not the only acceptable responses.

In the answer keys in the teacher presentation material, parentheses are used to indicate acceptable responses. The students' responses do not have to match the given wording to be appropriate.

Written Tasks

Most tasks in the program require written responses. These tasks provide a good test of whether the students understand the material that has just been presented in the exercise. As the students write their answers, quickly check their work.

Oral Tasks

For some tasks, the students read part of the material and then respond to an oral question or direction. (See Ⓓ in the analyzing arguments exercise just discussed.)

Some tasks specify individual turns. You are instructed to call on a student, or on individual students. (See Ⓔ in the analyzing arguments exercise.) Individual tasks usually involve a lengthy response, which would be difficult for the group to produce in unison, or a range of acceptable responses, which means that different students may produce different acceptable responses.

Other tasks do not specify whether you should call on an individual student. For these, you may call on a single student or you may call on the whole group. If you call on the group, precede the task by saying Everybody, what's the answer?

Signaling

When presenting group tasks, use signals to ensure that students respond together. By listening carefully, you can usually tell which students make mistakes, whether most members of the group have mastered a concept or skill, and whether the task should be repeated.

The general procedure for signaling is to present a cadence to the task, like the timing of a dance step. Everybody, what's a word that means the same thing? You may

snap your fingers, or tap your foot, or say Get ready as an extra cue for when the response is to occur.

For group responses, you should present the task in a way that permits all students to respond together in perfect unison. Keep the same cadence so that the students can easily respond to your signal without looking up or turning around to watch you.

Sample Formats

This section provides an overview of each of the skill categories. It indicates the major objectives, how the more prominent skills are taught, and briefly, how the category ties in with some skills taught in other categories.

Basic Tool: Using Sources of Information

Basic Comprehension Passages

The information source for each of these exercises is a passage that presents information or facts about a subject. Following the passage are questions about the material. Basic Information passages are presented throughout *Concept Applications*. On the following page is an example from Lesson 15 in the Student Book, along with the corresponding teacher presentation.

In step 2, you call on individual students to read part C. Permit each student to read two to five sentences. Then Say Okay or Stop and call on another student.

Step 2 indicates when you ask questions or give instructions. If you wish, you can add comments or questions; however, don't engage in substantial interruptions of the reading.

C Write **Part C** in the left margin of your paper. Then number it from 1 to 4. Ⓘ Read the story and answer the questions.

> Mr. Nelson was a nice old fellow, but he had one problem. He got his words mixed up. When he wanted to say **boar,** he said **sore.** When he wanted to say **sanded,** he said **banded.**
>
> Mr. Nelson loved to make little statues of animals. He made statues of geese, frogs, elephants, and dogs. One day he was working on a little wooden statue of a boar. (A boar is a wild pig with large tusks.) Mr. Nelson's granddaughter was watching him as he carved the boar and then sanded it. "Oh, it's starting to look really good," she said.
>
> "Yes," Mr. Nelson replied. "This sore will soon be banded."
>
> His granddaughter frowned. Then she smiled as she realized what he had meant to say. Ⓙ

1. What did Mr. Nelson mean when he said, "This sore will soon be banded"? *This boar will soon be sanded.*
2. How would Mr. Nelson say, "A sanded boar"? *A banded sore*
3. Name three kinds of animals that Mr. Nelson made statues of. *Any three—geese, frogs, elephants, dogs, boars*
4. What is a boar? Ⓚ *(A wild pig with large tusks)*

━━━━━ **EXERCISE 3** ━━━━━

STATEMENT INFERENCE
1. (Have the students find part C.)
2. (Call on individual students to read part C.)
   Ⓘ Do it now. (Wait.)
   Ⓙ Now we're going to read the questions. Don't write anything yet.
   Ⓚ Write the answers.
3. (Wait for the students to complete the items.) Let's check your answers. Put an **X** next to any item you miss.
4. (Call on individual students to read and answer each item.)

Steps 3 and 4 provide directions for checking answers.

Note that in the Student Book example, questions 3 and 4 require literal answers, whereas questions 1 and 2 require the student to make a deduction based on information given in the passage. Note, too, the use of parentheses in the answer key to indicate acceptable responses. The students' answers to question 4 may vary from the wording given and still be appropriate.

Words or Deductions

The work the students do with a written passage becomes more sophisticated later in the program, after they have practiced deductions. Beginning with Lesson 65, the students are required to classify the type of operation they used to arrive at an answer. Did they use words in the story to answer a question? Or did they perform a deduction that is based on words in the story? The example shown is the Workbook and teacher material in which Words or Deductions passages are introduced.

After students have worked on several passages in the carefully directed manner shown in the example, they work independently, reading passages, answering the questions, and indicating whether specified items are answered by words or by deductions. The independent work in Words or Deductions continues through Lesson 138.

Note: The students are not required to write the whole sentence for items that are answered by words in the passage. They may paraphrase the complete sentence, using a shorter sentence or even a phrase. As long as the student's answer is reasonable, the answer is correct. However, the students are to be instructed to underline an entire sentence when they are specifying the words that answer a question.

A Answers to some questions are based on words in a passage. Answers to other questions are based on deductions.

   If a question is answered by words in a passage, you can find those words.
   If a question is answered by a deduction, you cannot find the words. You must make up a deduction.
   Read this passage.

A hundred years ago, people were not concerned with ecology. They believed that there was no end to different types of wildlife. It seemed to them that it was impossible to kill all the ducks or all the buffaloes or all the leopards. So they killed ducks and leopards and buffaloes by the hundreds of thousands. When we look back on this killing, we may feel shocked. But for the people who lived a hundred years ago, wild animals seemed to be as plentiful as weeds. Nobody worried about killing these animals.

   The killing led to some animals becoming extinct. A type of animal becomes extinct when there are no more animals of that type. At one time, the passenger pigeon was a common bird. Today, the passenger pigeon is extinct. At one time, the Labrador duck was plentiful.

Today, this type of duck is extinct. Since the year 1800, over 100 species of animals have become extinct. This situation is very sad, because once an animal becomes extinct, it will never be seen on Earth again. Think of that. Although the passenger pigeon lived on Earth for over one hundred thousand years, you will never see a living passenger pigeon, nor will your children or grandchildren. The only type of passenger pigeon you will see is in a picture or in a museum.

* Here s a question:

   Why didn t people a hundred years ago worry about killing thousands of buffaloes?

What s the answer to that question? Ⓐ
If that question is answered by words in the passage, you can find those words.
Can you find the words? Ⓑ
So, is the question answered by words or by a deduction? Ⓒ

* Here s another question:

   What does it mean when we say that an animal is extinct?

What s the answer to that question? Ⓓ
If that question is answered by words in the passage, you can find those words.
Can you find the words? Ⓔ
So, is the question answered by words or by a deduction? Ⓕ

Write the answer to each question. For some items, you circle either **words** or **deduction.** If you circle **words,** underline the words in the passage that answer the item.

1. Why didn't people a hundred years ago worry about killing thousands of buffaloes?
(It seemed to them that it was impossible to kill all the ducks or all the buffaloes or all the leopards.)

Circle how the question is answered:
    (words)   deduction

2. What does it mean when we say that an animal is extinct?
(A type of animal becomes extinct when there are no more animals of that type.)

Circle how the question is answered:
    (words)   deduction

3. Why weren't people concerned with ecology a hundred years ago?
(They believed that there was no end to different types of wildlife.)

Circle how the question is answered:
    (words)   deduction

4. Name two animals that have become extinct.
(The passenger pigeon and the Labrador duck)

5. Will you ever see a live Labrador duck?
No

Circle how the question is answered:
    words   (deduction)

6. Why not?
(Because the Labrador duck is extinct)

7. Will you ever see a live passenger pigeon?
No

Circle how the question is answered:
    (words)   deduction

STATEMENT INFERENCE

1. (Have the students find Lesson 65, part A, in the **Workbook.**)

2. (Call on individual students to read up to Ⓕ.)

   Ⓐ (Call on a student.) Idea: It seemed to them that it was impossible to kill all the buffaloes.

   Ⓑ Everybody, look at the passage and see if you can find them. (Wait.) Can you find the words? *Yes.*

   Ⓒ What's the answer? *By words.*

   Ⓓ (Call on a student.) Idea: There are no more animals of that type.

   Ⓔ Everybody, look at the passage and see if you can find them. (Wait.) Can you find the words? *Yes.*

   Ⓕ What's the answer? *By words.*

3. Read the instructions and do the items. (Wait for the students to complete the items.) Let's check your answers. Put an **X** next to any item you miss.

4. (Call on individual students to read each item and the answer. If the item is answered by words in the passage, have the students tell which words they underlined.)

Beginning in Lesson 39, the students learn to use pictures as sources of information. The example below is a Student Book exercise from Lesson 39. The fact provides the students with background information. The precise answer to the first question, however, comes from the picture

---

★ **D** Write **Part D** in the left margin of your paper. Then number it 1 and 2. Here's a fact:

> **The ears of an African elephant are different from the ears of an Indian elephant.**

1. Look at the picture below and tell how the elephants' ears are different.
2. What kind of reference material would you use to support the fact?

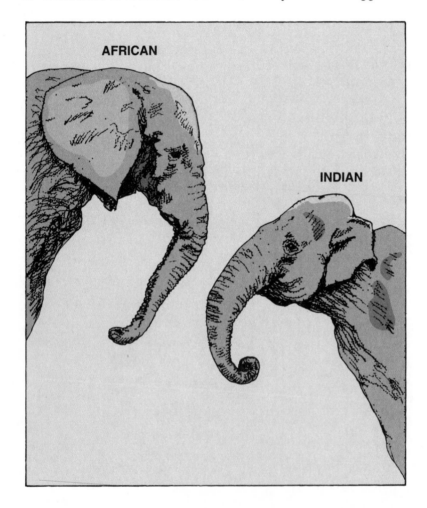

AFRICAN

INDIAN

The conventions for reading maps are introduced in Lesson 33. The example shown below is an early map exercise from the Student Book. In the map exercises, the students learn to answer questions about distances, populations, numbers of cities, names of rivers, and similar map information.

 D Each square on the map below is one kilometer long and one kilometer wide. Look at the map and answer the following questions.

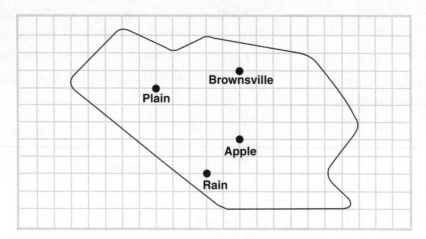

1. How far is it from Brownsville to Apple?
2. How far is it from Brownsville to Plain?
3. Is it farther from Brownsville to Apple or from Brownsville to Plain?

Graph reading begins in Lesson 67 of the Workbook. The students are presented with different types of graphs: line, circle, and bar. The information graphed is also varied: income, growth, temperature, production, and so on. The following example shows the first graph-interpretation exercise.

 A To read a graph, you use two sets of numbers. One set is up and down, and the other set is across the bottom. Look at the graph below.

The up-and-down numbers on this graph stand for years. Circle the word **years** at the top of the graph.

The letter **D** is on the graph. That letter is next to the year 1982. Put the letter **A** next to the year 1988.
Put the letter **B** next to the year 1994.
Put the letter **C** where the year 1985 would be. That s halfway between 1984 and 1986.

The numbers at the bottom of the graph tell about the number of fish caught. Circle the words **number of fish caught** at the bottom of the graph.

The letter **F** is on the graph. That letter is right above 3000 fish. Put the letter **M** right above 7000 fish.

Put the letter **P** right above 1000 fish.
Put the letter **R** right above 8000 fish.

Find the letter **H**.
H shows the number of fish caught in one year. To find the year for **H**, go this way: ←. What year is **H** next to?
To find the number of fish caught for **H**, go this way: ↓.
How many fish is **H** above?
So, **H** shows 4000 fish caught in 1988.

Find the letter **G**.
G shows the number of fish caught in one year. To find the year for **G**, which way do you go? What year is **G** next to?
To find the number of fish caught for **G**, which way do you go?
How many fish is **G** above?
So, **G** shows 6000 fish caught in 1984.

Find the letter **J**.
J shows the number of fish caught in one year. To find the year for **J**, which way do you go? What year is **J** next to?
To find the number of fish caught for **J**, which way do you go?
How many fish is **J** above?
So, **J** shows 10,000 fish caught in 1992.

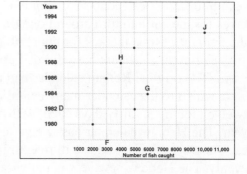

Supporting Evidence

After the students learn about using three types of reference books—a dictionary, atlas, and encyclopedia—they are presented with exercises in which they are given a fact. They are to indicate the type of reference book most appropriate for finding evidence that supports that fact. Later, they are provided with a map or a passage that supports a given fact and from which they must get further information.

Beginning with Lesson 87, exercises present two sources of information that describe a particular topic. These may be a graph and a passage, a map and a passage, or two passages. The students indicate which source answers specific questions.

The final type of exercise involving supporting information is introduced in Lesson 104 of the Student Book. As shown in the example below, the students are presented with two passages that contradict each other on several points. After the students identify the points of disagreement, they learn to consult reference material to help decide which account is accurate.

The two passages below contradict each other on two important points. Make sure you find those contradictions when you read the passages.

Passage 1. The new year for all calendars has always begun in January. The Roman calendar originally had twelve months and began with January. The Egyptian calendar also had twelve months. There were some problems with the original Roman calendar, but most of these were resolved by Julius Caesar, who adjusted the length of the months so that the year was 365 days. Julius Caesar also introduced a leap year every four years. In a leap year, there is an extra day.

The names of some of the months from the early Roman calendar are with us today—September, October, November, and December. These names mean the seventh month, eighth month, ninth month, and tenth month. Julius Caesar renamed the fifth month after himself—July. The ruler who followed as his successor, Augustus Caesar, renamed the sixth month after himself—August.

Passage 2. A calendar is a way of dividing up time so that people can keep track of time in the same way. Throughout history, there have been several different calendars. For example, one day is the amount of time it takes for the earth to turn around one time. A year, which is 365 days long, is the amount of time it takes for the earth to travel around the sun one time.

Different calendars have divided up the days of the year in different ways. The original Roman calendar had ten months—January and February were added to the calendar many centuries later. The Egyptian calendar had twelve months of thirty days each, with five days tacked on to the end of the year. The Hebrew calendar has twelve months of twenty-nine or thirty days each and occasionally adds a thirteenth month to make the calendar come out evenly. The Hebrew new year is in the fall to coincide with the estimated date of Creation.

The passages contradict each other on two important points. What are those points?

Let's look up **calendar** in a dictionary or encyclopedia and find out which passage is accurate.

Basic Tool: Communicating Information

The skills taught in this category develop vocabulary and writing ability.

Definitions

Presenting dictionary definitions is typically not a very effective way to introduce new words to students. For a student to use a word, the student must understand something about the meaning of the word (which familiar words it stands for) and how it is used (which words go with it).

A dictionary definition usually labels the part of speech of a word (such as verb, intransitive). It may also indicate words that accompany the word being defined (e.g., This word is usually used with the word **with**). However, the student receives almost no experience in dealing with sentences that contain the word.

The strategy for teaching word meanings in *Concept Applications* is through model sentences. Each sentence contains a number of useful vocabulary words. The students learn what the words mean, and then they practice substituting the new vocabulary words for their synonyms in other sentences. The following example is the first Definitions exercise, which is in Lesson 18 of the Student Book.

The model sentence below contains vocabulary words that you will use in other sentences. You're going to memorize the model sentence. Make sure that you know what the words mean and how to spell them.

Here's the model sentence:

> **By hesitating, she lost her opportunity.**

Here's what it means:

> **By pausing, she lost her chance.**

Study the model sentence until you can say it without looking at it.
What does the word **hesitating** mean?
What does the word **opportunity** mean?
What's another way of saying, **By pausing, she lost her chance?**

For each item, say a sentence that means the same thing.

1. Although he paused, he did not give up his chance.
2. Tom had four chances to buy that house.

The following chart lists the model sentences, along with their meaning as presented in the program. It also indicates the lesson in which each model sentence is introduced.

Lesson	Sentence
18	By *hesitating,* she lost her *opportunity.* By *pausing,* she lost her *chance.*
21	His directions were *ambiguous* and *redundant.* His directions were *unclear* and *repetitive.*
27	They *converted* their Swiss *currency* into Canadian *currency.* They *changed* their Swiss *money* into Canadian *money.*
33	The *regulation restricted* their parking. The *rule limited* their parking.
56	Her *response* was *replete* with *extraneous* details. Her *answer* was *filled* with *irrelevant* details.
62	They *devised* an *appropriate strategy.* They *made up* a *fitting plan.*
85	A strange *phenomenon* caused the *anxiety* that she *exhibited.* A strange *event* caused the *fear* that she *showed.*
101	The major *contended* that he had *valid motives* for *concealing* the *data.* The major *argued* that he had *sound reasons* for *hiding* the *facts.*

In another Definitions activity, the student is given a passage to rewrite. There are places indicated where the new vocabulary words can be substituted for words in the passage. By Lesson 122 in the Student Book, the students are applying new vocabulary skills.

New vocabulary is also presented in a manner similar to that encountered in everyday reading. A word is introduced, a sentence or two is used to define the word, and the word is used in still another sentence. In Lesson 90 in the Student Book, the words introduced are **clarity, cautious,** and **sorrow;** these are used later in other activities. The program introduces 26 vocabulary words in this way: **clarity, cautious, sorrow, rogue, sanctioned, scrupulous, somnolent, indolent, lethal, preceding, vital, extrovert, genius, subsequent, tightwad, emphatically, independent, proximity, catastrophe, inquiries, temporary, affirmed, audibly, imitation, remote,** and **wildlife.**

Vocabulary Testing

Starting in Lesson 25, vocabulary testing occurs every five lessons. For these tests, the students write the model sentences that they have learned.

Combining Sentences

Even if students understand the meaning of all the words, they may fail to comprehend certain sentences if they do not understand the conventions of syntax. Typically, students have trouble with sentences that do not occur in everyday conversations—sentences with words such as **therefore** and **however.** The Combining Sentences exercises show students how more complex sentences are created from simple parts.

The students are first taught that consistent sentences may be combined with the words **and, so,** and **therefore.** Inconsistent sentences may be combined with **however** and **but.** The following example from Lesson 16 in the Student Book reviews the words used to combine consistent sentences.

What kind of sentence tells something we don't expect to happen?
What kind of sentence tells something we expect to happen?
To combine two sentences that seem consistent, we can use the word **and,** the word **so,** or the word **therefore.**

Here's what we know:

> **Gino loves to work outside.**

Here's a sentence that seems consistent with the sentence in the box:
> **He got a job as a gardener.**

Here are the two sentences combined with the word **and:**
> **Gino loves to work outside, and he got a job as a gardener.**

Here are the two sentences combined with the word **so:**
> **Gino loves to work outside, so he got a job as a gardener.**

Here are the two sentences combined with the word **therefore:**
> **Gino loves to work outside; therefore, he got a job as a gardener.**

Here's what we know:

> **Jolene's family is very poor.**

Read the sentence below and find the one that seems consistent with the sentence in the box.

- **She works every day after school.**
- **She spends a lot of money on clothes.**

Use the word **and** to combine the sentence in the box with the consistent sentence.
Use the word **so** to combine the sentence in the box with the consistent sentence.
Use the word **therefore** to combine the sentence in the box with the consistent sentence.

Beginning with Lesson 48, the students are taught how the words **which** and **who** function in sentences. In Lesson 63 in the Student Book, the students practice converting a sentence into a clause by substituting **which** or **who** for the underlined part. Finally, in Lesson 65, students combine sentences using **who** and **which.**

Sentence-combination skills are reinforced in a variety of application exercises as well as in editing tasks. This ensures the retention of these skills.

Editing

Typically, after a new skill in Communicating Information has been taught, editing exercises involving that skill are presented. In addition to the editing exercises involving definitions and contradictions, the students practice editing passages for more common mistakes. Subject-verb agreement is introduced in Lesson 1. The example from Lesson 13 in the Student Book provides practice on **is-are** when the word **each** is used. The students learn the correct usage of **was-were** from a format similar to this one.

Next, the students edit passages in which **is** and **are** are used incorrectly. A similar series of formats teaches correct usage of **has and have.**

Another skill that is taught in editing is identifying parts of sentences that are redundant. The students explain the redundancy by completing an **if-then** statement, such as **If you know that it will be sent without charge, you already know that it's a free gift.** Some words involved in these exercises are vocabulary words from the Definitions exercises.

Remember, the word **each** tells about one thing, not more than one thing.
So **each** goes with the verb **is** or the verb **was.**

This is correct:	**The soldiers are tired.**
But this is not correct:	**Each of the soldiers are tired.**
This is correct:	**Each of the soldiers is tired.**

Say each sentence below with the verb **is** or the verb **are.**

1. The girls _____ hungry.
2. The dogs _____ running.
3. The men _____ happy.
4. Each of the girls _____ hungry.
5. Each of the dogs _____ running.
6. Each of the men _____ happy.

Meaning from Context

Beginning in Lesson 104, the students are taught to analyze sentences for unintended meanings. The introductory exercise is shown in the example below.

 Each sentence below has two possible meanings. One is the meaning that the author intends. The other meaning is an unintended meaning.

- **Everybody around the racetrack cheered as the man beat the greyhound dog.**

Here's the intended meaning of the sentence:

The man ran faster than the dog.

Here's the unintended meaning of the sentence:

The man hit the dog.

The two meanings are possible because one word in the sentence can have two meanings. Which word is that?

Here's another sentence:

- **When the final buzzer sounded, the Vikings were on top of the Braves.**

What's the intended meaning of the sentence?
What's the unintended meaning?
Which words are involved in the two meanings?

In another series of exercises, an ambiguous sentence is followed by one that clarifies the intended meaning. The students must infer the intended meaning of the first sentence from the information provided by the second sentence.

Beginning with Lesson 95, the students read a passage that contains an underlined word. The context of the passage makes the meaning of this word obvious. For example, a passage uses the word **ebullient** and describes how joyfully a person acted. All new words introduced in the Meaning from Context activities appear in the student glossary. However, the students are **not** to use their glossaries during these activities. Remind the students that they must figure out the meaning from the passage. Also, for the items that require the students to write a sentence from the passage that contradicts specific ideas, the students are to write complete sentences. They do not, however, have to write sentences that contain the new word.

The final series of exercises in determining meaning from context begins in Lesson 131. The students read a passage that describes a change that came about. The cause of the change is not specified, but must be inferred from the passage. It is assumed that what is written has been selected because it is relevant to the outcome or change. This skill is very important in understanding all kinds of writing—from poetry to military history. The details that are presented are not just randomly selected, even though the passage may not tell how each is related to the outcome. The fact that these details are included in the passage suggests that they are relevant.

Basic Tool: Using Information for Directions

This group of activities deals with the precise use of language to convey instructions. There are three types of activities.

1 Writing directions for a simple diagram

2 Filling out forms by using the factual information provided

3 Recognizing discrepancies between instructions for creating a diagram and the diagram itself

The skills that are taught in this category are used in other categories. The students underline, correct, fill in blanks, cross out, and follow similar directions in various exercises throughout the program.

Writing Directions

The students begin writing directions for simple diagrams in Lesson 4. They have been taught the words **horizontal, vertical,** and **slanted.** The students must focus on writing instructions that tell **what** to make and **where** to make it.

Filling Out Forms

The students use the factual information that is provided to complete some common types of forms, such as an application for a student loan or a new job. The introductory exercise appears in Lesson 11.

Identifying Contradictory Directions

These exercises require students to examine a diagram, circle the instruction the diagram contradicts, and draw a new diagram that is consistent with the instructions. The introductory exercise appears in Lesson 25.

Higher-Order Skill: Organizing Information

This category focuses on skills related to handling systems of related information.

Main Idea

The introductory Main Idea exercises show the learner that some sentences provide additional information about a main-idea sentence, while some sentences do not. The following example is from Lesson 61 in the Student Book.

 Paragraphs sometimes have a main-idea sentence. It's the sentence that tells what the paragraph is about.
Here's the main-idea sentence for a paragraph:

> **The collision occurred at 2 A.M.**

Read the sentence to yourself and get ready to say it.

Tell if each sentence below provides more information about the main idea.

- **Two cars collided at the intersection of Fourth and Grand.**
Does that sentence provide more information about the main idea?

- **The river was beautiful in the moonlight.**
Does that sentence provide more information about the main idea?

- **One car, a red sports car, was driven by Emil Brock.**
Does that sentence provide more information about the main idea?

A variation of this exercise presents main-idea sentences for two different paragraphs. Additional sentences are then presented. The students determine which paragraph each of these sentences belongs to. The introductory exercise from Lesson 66 in the Student Book is shown in the following example.

 B

Here are two main ideas.
Main idea for paragraph 1:

> **Frank was getting ready to go fishing.**

Main idea for paragraph 2:

> **Frank had an accident and nearly drowned.**

Each of the following sentences belongs to either paragraph 1 or paragraph 2. Read each sentence. Then tell which paragraph the sentence belongs to:

• **His pole fell in the water and he jumped in after it.**
Which paragraph does that sentence belong to?

He got his boots and gear ready the night before.
Which paragraph does that sentence belong to?

He told his mother he would bring some trout home for dinner.
Which paragraph does that sentence belong to?

His clothes became heavy with water and dragged him to the bottom of the stream.
Which paragraph does that sentence belong to?

Holding his breath, he took off his boots and struggled out of his clothes.
Which paragraph does that sentence belong to?

He went to bed early so that he could get an early start the next morning.
Which paragraph does that sentence belong to?

He bought some new hooks and lures.
Which paragraph does that sentence belong to?

He swam to the surface and gasped for air.
Which paragraph does that sentence belong to?

The stream carried him under some low-hanging branches, which he grabbed onto.
Which paragraph does that sentence belong to?

He dragged himself out of the water and lay panting on the bank of the stream.
Which paragraph does that sentence belong to?

He had marked the places where he wanted to fish on some maps.
Which paragraph does that sentence belong to?

A variety of similar exercises demonstrate the relationship between a main-idea sentence and sentences that tell more about the main idea. Beginning in Lesson 73 in the Student Book, the students are given one main-idea sentence. They read three different passages and select the one for which the main idea is appropriate. Note that each of these passages deals with the same basic topic and contains the same vocabulary. Also, each passage begins with the same sentence. The students are therefore required to attend to the relevant details of the passages.

In the final Main Idea exercises, the students match three main-idea sentences with three different passages.

Outlining

The Main Idea exercises are prerequisites for outlining. A main-idea sentence expresses the main thing that is being said. Sentences that say more about the main thing are points that belong under the main idea. The students are introduced to the conventions for outlining in Lesson 91 of the Student Book. As shown in the example on the following page, the first part of the activity presents the main idea for the passage and the actual format for creating the outline, which the students copy. In the second part of the activity, the main idea is given, but the students must complete the outline.

Write **Part B** in the left margin of your paper. Read the passage below.

> You will probably have many job interviews during your life. Knowing how to be interviewed is very important. You will do well on a job interview if you remember certain things. Here are a few pointers to keep in mind when you're being interviewed. First, make sure that your clothes are neat and well pressed. They don't have to be expensive or high-fashion clothes—just clean and ironed. If you look as if you care about yourself, the employer will think you will care about your job. The second thing to remember is to be on time for the interview. If you arrive late, your chances of getting hired are probably pretty small. A third point is to find out as much about the job as you can during the interview. Ask what kind of work you will be doing and what you will be paid. Ask about benefits, such as insurance and vacations. The last thing to remember is to be relaxed during an interview. Many people are so nervous when they are interviewed that the employer thinks they can't do the job. So if you smile, relax, and ask questions, your chances of getting hired are very good.

The main idea of the passage you just read is: **What to do on a job interview.**

The author gives four tips on what you should do on a job interview. The first tip is: **Make sure your clothes are clean and neat.** What are the other three tips?

Copy the main idea and the four points on your paper just as they appear in the outline below. Label the main idea roman numeral one. To show that the points are under the main idea, indent them and label them **A, B, C,** and **D.**

I. What to do on a job interview
   A. Make sure your clothes are neat and clean
   B. Arrive on time
   C. Find out as much about the job as you can
   D. Be relaxed

Read the passage below.

> Small details are very important when you apply for credit. An important reason that people are not given credit has to do with their handwriting. They write illegibly. The writing may be so poor that the credit manager cannot figure out where the person lives. The credit manager may not even be able to figure out who sent in the form. Sometimes the credit manager looks at the sloppy handwriting and concludes that if the person who is applying for credit does not take care in filling out the form, that person will not take care in repaying the loan.

The main idea of the passage is: **What can happen if you write illegibly on a credit application.** The author makes three points that fall under the main idea. Write the main idea and the three points in outline form. Label the points **A, B,** and **C,** and indent them under the main idea.

In later Outlining exercises, the students are given a passage and three alternatives for the main idea. First, they must read the passage and choose the appropriate main idea. Then they must outline the passage. The introductory exercise appears in Lesson 101 of the Student Book.

Specific-General

The most difficult main-idea concept for students is the main-idea sentence that does not correspond to any sentence in the passage—the sentence that provides a general summary of the information contained in the passage. To help the students grasp this concept, they work on a series of exercises in which they must produce a new statement that is more general or more specific than the one provided. The introductory exercise, in which the students begin to learn how to make a statement more general, appears in Lesson 112.

To make a statement more general, you use the names of larger classes.
Here's a statement:
> **The fourteen-year-old boy walked into the little coffee shop.**

You can make the statement more general by using the name of a larger class for each underlined part.
Here's a more general statement:
> **The teenager walked into the store.**

Here's a statement that is even more general:
> **The person walked into the building.**

- Here's a new statement:
> **That cocker spaniel is curled up in a red station wagon.**

Make up a more general statement by using the name of a larger class for each underlined part.

- Here's a new statement:
> **Oranges are often put in fruit crates.**

Make up a more general statement by using the name of a larger class for each underlined part.

- Here's a new statement:
> **Sheep, goats, cows, horses, and deer on my farm like to eat grass and bushes.**

Make up a more general statement by using the name of a larger class for each underlined part.

In the next exercise, the students are required to compare a statement with a picture and write a statement that is more specific than the one provided.

The final exercise begins in Lesson 121. The students are given statements. With each statement are instructions for writing a new statement that is either more specific or more general.

Morals

Morals are treated as special kinds of main ideas. The program defines a moral as a general statement about specific events described in a passage. The students learn how to identify the specific events in a passage that illustrate a moral, as well as to generalize from specific events to formulate a moral. The first exercises present a passage with the moral stated. The students must supply the specific events described in the passage that illustrate the moral. The following example shows the introductory activity in Lesson 121 of the Student Book.

Some passages present a main idea that is called a moral. When a passage presents a moral, the passage presents specific events. The moral is a general statement about those events.

The passage below presents this moral:

If you try, you'll succeed.

> Irma started out as the poorest high jumper on the track team. Her best jump was slightly more than three feet. But Irma wanted to be a star high jumper. So she practiced, listened, and talked to herself. She watched the better jumpers—watched the way they approached the bar, how they tossed their arms when they started over the bar, and how they moved their legs. She listened to the coach when he explained jumping techniques to other jumpers. She arrived at practice early every day, and she worked and worked. At the end of her first season, she was better. She approached the bar faster, she had a better takeoff, and she tossed her arms with more force. She could now clear one and one-half meters, which isn't bad. But, by the end of the second season, Irma could clear six feet. She placed second in the state. You might say that she had the ability all along, but Irma also worked very hard.

Name the specific events in the story that show Irma tried.
Name the specific events in the story that show Irma succeeded.

Beginning in Lesson 125, the students read a passage and select the most appropriate moral for the passage from a group of three alternatives. And in Lesson 129, the students are required to make up morals for passages. At this point, the students have a good idea of how a general statement can be used to sum up specific events.

Visual-Spatial Organization

For several reasons, visual-spatial displays are powerful mnemonic devices that aid in the retrieval of related information:

◆ There is a visual representation of each major point and each point that comes under a major heading.

◆ Any given label on the display can be retrieved by starting at different parts of the display and working toward the label in question.

◆ The memory system used to retrieve information from visual-spatial displays is different from the memory used for retrieving information presented through language.

A visual-spatial way of organizing information is introduced in Lesson 84 of the Workbook. As shown in the example below, the display deals with facts about different types of animals.

In subsequent lessons, new information is added, and the students are tested regularly on the display. The final form of the display

7. The passage names three types of carnivores. One type is the predator. Fill in the boxes below for the other two types.

• Below the box for predators, list six kinds of predators.

• Below the other two boxes, list two examples of each kind of animal.

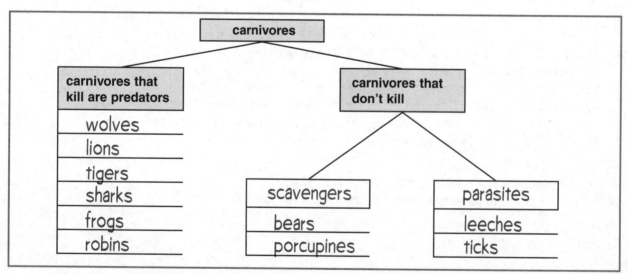

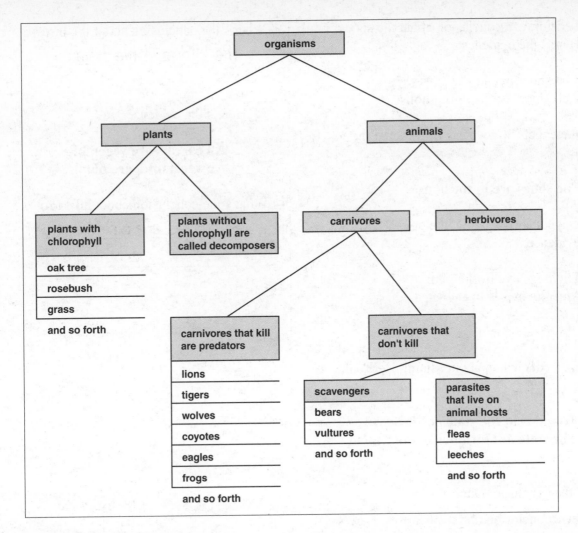

is introduced in Lesson 119. As shown above, the display now reflects the organization of both plants and animals.

Higher-Order Skill: Operating on Information

This category concentrates on procedures for operating on passages or arguments. It provides answers to questions such as "How do you determine whether a conclusion is valid?" "How do you evaluate the evidence an author presents?" and "How do you evaluate an author's appeals?"

Clearly, the answers to these questions are among the most important comprehension skills. The skills taught in Operating on Information are survival skills useful to anyone who is exposed to advertisers, interest groups, politicians, salespeople, journalists, and so on. Politicians appeal to what people should do; ads seem to offer proof when no proof is actually given; used-car salespeople present unsound but appealing arguments; the editorial page in a newspaper tries to shape opinions about world events. To survive intelligently, a student should understand these forces and recognize when an appeal is unsound.

Deductions

Deductions have been stressed throughout the earlier levels of the Comprehension programs. The emphasis on deductions continues in *Concept Applications* because most arguments hinge on deduction.

The example on the next page shows the basic Deduction exercise introduced in Lesson 1 of the Workbook.

Let's draw a conclusion about the shoes. Here's the evidence:

The shoes are in the closet.
And the closet is in the house.

Here's the conclusion we can draw about the shoes:

The shoes are in the house.

- Draw a conclusion about the dogs. Here's the evidence:

  The dogs are in the pen.
  And the pen is in the yard.

What's the conclusion about the dogs?

- Draw a conclusion about Miami. Here's the evidence:

  Miami is in the state of Florida.
  The state of Florida is in the United States.

What's the conclusion about Miami?

- Draw a conclusion about all carrots. Here's the evidence:

  All carrots are vegetables.
  All vegetables are plants.

What's the conclusion about all carrots?

Read the evidence and write the conclusion for each item.

1. Here's the evidence:

  The bird is in the nest.
  And the nest is in the tree.

What's the conclusion about the bird?

The bird is in the tree.

What's the conclusion about the bird?

The bird is in the tree.

2. Here's the evidence:

  All carrots are vegetables.
  All vegetables are plants.

What's the conclusion about all carrots?

All carrots are plants.

Next, the students work with deductions that lead to a **maybe** conclusion. They learn that the rule in this type of deduction contains the word **some.**

Some sheep are black.
Bibo is a sheep.
So, maybe Bibo is black.

Diagrams are also used to demonstrate further the logic of deductions. These exercises are introduced in Lesson 6 of the Workbook. A verbal explanation of how **maybe** conclusions work is sometimes quite involved: If all the dots are in the circle and if part of the circle is in the square, **not every dot that is in the circle is necessarily in the square.** As shown in the example on the next page, the use of the diagrams simplifies this explanation and makes the relationships obvious.

Look at diagram 1.

Diagram 1

You can't see the dots, but **all the dots are in the circle.**

Here's a deduction that is based on the diagram:

> All the dots are in the circle.
> The circle is in the square.
> So, all the dots are in the square.

To check the conclusion, draw dots in diagram 1 so that all the dots are in the circle.

Is the conclusion correct? Are all the dots in the square?

• Look at diagram 2.

Diagram 2

You can't see the dots, but all the dots are in the triangle.

Complete the deduction based on the diagram:

All the dots are in the triangle.
The triangle is in the square.

So, _____

_____

Draw the dots in diagram 2.

• Look at diagram 3.

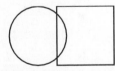

Diagram 3

You can't see the dots, but **all the dots are in the circle.**

Here's the deduction that is based on the diagram:

> All the dots are in the circle.
> Part of the circle is in the square.
> So, maybe all the dots are in the square.

Look at diagram A and diagram B. Diagram A shows where the dots could be if all the dots were in the square. Diagram B shows where the dots could be if only some of the dots were in the square.

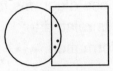   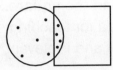

Diagram A   **Diagram B**

We want to draw a conclusion about all the dots. We don't know which diagram is correct, so we draw this conclusion:

Maybe all the dots are in the square.

• Look at diagram 4.

Diagram 4

You can't see the dots, but **all the dots are in the circle.**

Draw a conclusion about all the dots:

All the dots are in the circle.
Part of the circle is in the triangle.

So, _____

_____

Complete diagram C and diagram D.
For diagram C, show where the dots could be if all the dots were in the triangle. For diagram D, show where the dots could be if only some of the dots were in the triangle.

Diagram C   **Diagram D**

In Lesson 8, diagrams are introduced to teach students about class exclusion: **If all the dots are in the circle and none of the circle is in the square, none of the dots can be in the square.** These diagrams form the basis for teaching skills related to relevant and irrelevant information.

Beginning with Lesson 35 in the Student Book, the students are introduced to the idea that the first statement presented as evidence may be a rule. The rule is followed by additional evidence. As shown in the example, by using the rule and the additional evidence, you can draw a conclusion. Note that this form of deduction is the one that is used in science.

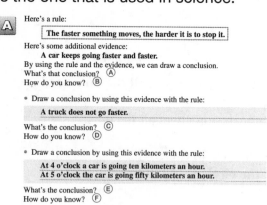

The next series of activities introduces evidence that is irrelevant to the conclusion. The students are given a rule and several pieces of additional evidence. First, they must indicate whether the evidence is relevant or irrelevant to the rule. If the evidence is relevant, they state the conclusion. If the evidence is irrelevant, they indicate that no conclusion can be drawn.

A Here's a rule:

> **All soccer players have strong legs.**

Tell if each piece of evidence below is **relevant** to the rule or **irrelevant** to the rule. Remember, if it is irrelevant, you can't draw a conclusion. Here are the pieces of evidence:

1. **Lisa's favorite sport is skindiving.**
   Is this evidence relevant or irrelevant? Ⓐ
   So what's the conclusion? Ⓑ
2. **Carlos plays soccer.**
   Is this evidence relevant or irrelevant? Ⓒ
   So what's the conclusion? Ⓓ
3. **Margo goes skiing every weekend.**
   Is this evidence relevant or irrelevant? Ⓔ
   So what's the conclusion? Ⓕ
4. **Nanda has played in six soccer tournaments.**
   Is this evidence relevant or irrelevant? Ⓖ
   So what's the conclusion? Ⓗ

Basic Evidence

In the Deduction activities, information that leads to a conclusion is treated as evidence. The emphasis of these activities is on drawing a conclusion. In contrast, the focus of Basic Evidence exercises is on the evidence. The students decide which evidence, if any, supports a conclusion. The evidence may be presented indirectly (derived through inference), or it may be embedded in a passage. The initial exercises, however, present evidence quite directly. Different facts (evidence) are presented, followed by several conclusions. The students must decide which fact best explains each conclusion.

These exercises involve using an unstated rule to help form a deduction. Figuring out the answer would involve this kind of deductive reasoning:

People who like to play sports need shoes.
Susan likes to play sports.
Therefore, Susan needs shoes.
(Therefore, she bought five pairs of tennis shoes.)

After the students have learned about irrelevant evidence, an exercise is introduced in which they judge whether evidence is relevant or irrelevant to the facts provided.

 You're going to use facts as evidence to explain why different things may happen. Here are the facts:

Fact A.	**Susan liked to play sports.**
Fact B.	**Susan was a lawyer.**
Fact C.	**Susan was not tall.**

Read the facts over until you can say them without looking. (H)

1. Here's what happened: **Susan never played center in basketball.** Say the fact that best explains why that happened. (I)
2. Here's what happened: **She bought five pairs of tennis shoes.** Say the fact that best explains why that happened. (J)
3. Here's what happened: **She knew the judge in Lincoln City.** Say the fact that best explains why that happened. (K)
4. Here's what happened: **She kept her baseball equipment in the garage.** Say the fact that best explains why that happened. (L)

For each item, write the **letter of the fact** that best explains what happened. (M)

5. She never played center in basketball. __C__
6. She bought five pairs of tennis shoes. __A__
7. She knew the judge in Lincoln City. __B__
8. She kept her baseball equipment in the garage. __A__
9. She stood on a stool to reach the shelves. __C__

In Lesson 31, a series of exercises begins that consist of a passage followed by conclusions. In the first exercise, which is shown in the following example, the students determine which sentence in the passage supports each conclusion.

Note that the evidence does not translate literally. The passage does not state that a *mature* hiccup fish is longer than you are. Rather, it states that a fully grown (equals *mature*) hiccup fish is 4 meters long (equals *longer than you are*). The students must figure out these equivalences to find the appropriate evidence.

B Read the following passage.

> The hiccup fish of Brazil swallows huge gulps of air and makes a hiccuping sound when the air is released. A fully grown fish is four meters long. Its hiccup can be heard more than a kilometer away.

Here is a conclusion based on the passage:

A mature hiccup fish is longer than you are.

The evidence that supports this conclusion is in one of the sentences. Which sentence is that?

Here is another conclusion:

The hiccup fish sometimes comes to the surface of the water.

The evidence that supports this conclusion is in one of the sentences. Which sentence is that?

In Lesson 43, a variation of the exercise just discussed is introduced. In this exercise, the passage may contain evidence that refutes or contradicts some conclusions.

• Here s a conclusion:

The trees on a hillside serve no useful purpose.

Does the passage contain evidence to support this conclusion or evidence to contradict this conclusion? (H)
The evidence in the passage contradicts the conclusion. So we can say that the evidence **refutes** the conclusion. Which sentence in the passage refutes the conclusion? (I)

• Here s another conclusion:

More young trees may survive on flat land.

Does the passage contain evidence to support this conclusion or evidence to refute this conclusion? (J)
Which sentence contains the evidence? (K)

In Basic Evidence, the students learn two tests for determining whether evidence is relevant to a rule. Consider this rule: **Trees are stationary.** According to the first test, evidence is relevant if it tells that something **is** a tree. The second test, which follows, is introduced in Lesson 69. According to this test, evidence is relevant if it tells that something **is not** stationary. By applying these tests, the students have a precise way of telling why evidence is irrelevant.

When the students complete the exercises in Basic Evidence, they have the skills needed to evaluate the internal structure of an argument to see whether it is sound with respect to evidence. They have learned how to see whether there is evidence to support the conclusion, how to identify this evidence, and how to determine whether the evidence is relevant.

Argument Rules

These activities, like Basic Evidence, deal with the internal structure of arguments. Important rules are presented for making arguments that are sound.

The exercises beginning in Lesson 36 teach students to identify a conclusion that is not actually stated, but that is clearly indicated by the evidence the argument presents. The following example is from Lesson 37.

Read each argument and tell what the conclusion is.

> **I'm not voting in the presidential election this year.**
> **What's the point? The last election was rigged anyway.**

What does the writer of this argument want us to conclude?

• Here's another argument:

> **My car's been sounding funny ever since I bought gas at that new station. I don't think I'll give them any more business.**

What does the writer of this argument want us to conclude?

The first rule for sound arguments is introduced in Lesson 42. The argument shown in the example below is faulty because it breaks the rule.

Here's a new rule:

> **Just because two things happen around the same time doesn't mean that one thing causes the other thing.**

Read the rule over to yourself and get ready to say it.

The argument below is faulty because it breaks the rule.
Read the argument.

> **I went to Chicago, and it rained in Chicago. I went to Cleveland, and it rained in Cleveland. So I think I'll go to New York City and make it rain there.**

What does the writer want us to conclude?
Why does the writer think that going to a city causes rain?
Say the rule the argument breaks.

Here's how you could prove that going to a city could not cause rain. Send the person to lots of cities. If it doesn't rain **every time** the person goes to one of those cities, going to the city does not cause rain.

Other rules are introduced similarly. The chart below lists the rules and the number of the lesson in which each rule is introduced.

Rule	Lesson
Rule 1. Just because two things happen around the same time doesn't mean one thing causes the other thing.	42
Rule 2. Just because you know about a part doesn't mean you know about the whole thing.	46
Rule 3. Just because you know about a part doesn't mean you know about another part.	61
Rule 4. Just because you know about a whole thing doesn't mean you know about every part.	61
Rule 5. Just because words are the same doesn't mean they have the same meaning.	67
Rule 6. Just because the writer presents some choices doesn't mean there aren't other choices.	78
Rule 7. Just because events have happened in the past doesn't mean they'll always happen.	122

After the students have been introduced to a new rule, they work on discrimination exercises in which they must identify the rule that is broken by each argument. By Lesson 65 in the program, four rules have been introduced.

In addition to expressing the rules that arguments break, the students apply the rules to concrete situations. First they indicate the intended conclusion of an argument. Then they specify a test for determining the validity of that argument.

Special emphasis is placed on the rule **Just because words are the same doesn't mean they have the same meaning.** Violations of this rule are often difficult to detect, yet, as shown in the example below from Lesson 71, they can make the most unsound arguments seem plausible.

D Read the argument below and answer the questions.

Sam said his tree had a lovely bark. I had no idea that trees could make sounds like dogs.

1. What does the writer want us to conclude?

   (Sam's tree barks like a dog.)

2. What do you point out to show that the argument is faulty?

   (Part of the evidence has more than one meaning.)

3. What evidence has more than one meaning?

   The word "bark"

4. Write a conclusion that is based on the other meaning of that evidence.

   (Sam said his tree had a lovely outer covering.)

Ought Statements

In Lesson 91, arguments that involve the words **ought** and **should** are introduced. The initial exercises require the students to discriminate between statements of ought and statements of fact. (**People should eat the right kind of food** is a statement of ought. **People ate the right kind of food** is a statement of fact.)

Beginning with Lesson 105, the students are taught to distinguish between a statement of ought and a statement of fact that involves statistics. (**Nearly everybody agreed that murder is evil** is a statement of fact.)

Beginning with Lesson 106, the students learn a rule about drawing conclusions that are statements of ought: **If the conclusion is a statement of ought, the rule at the beginning of the deduction must be a statement of ought.** Part of the introductory format is shown in the example below.

 Some arguments end with a conclusion that is a statement of ought. Here's a rule about conclusions that are statements of ought:

> **If the conclusion is a statement of ought, the rule at the beginning of the deduction must be a statement of ought.**

Here's a valid deduction:
You ought to do what your mother tells you to do.
Your mother tells you to do your homework.
Therefore, you ought to do your homework.
The conclusion is a statement of ought and the rule at the beginning of the deduction is a statement of ought. The deduction is valid.

Here's a deduction with the rule missing:
If you stay slim, you'll live longer.
Therefore, you should stay slim.
The conclusion is a statement of ought, so what do you know about the rule at the beginning of the deduction?
Here's that rule: **You should do things that let you live longer.**
Say the whole deduction.

Here's another deduction with the rule missing:
If you exercise, you'll stay in good health.
Therefore, you ought to exercise.
The conclusion is a statement of ought, so what do you know about the missing rule?
Figure out the missing rule.
Say the whole deduction.

In this type of exercise, the students apply the missing rule. The skill is important because it is frequently used in figuring out a writer's assumptions when they are unstated.

As shown in the following example, the students next learn that although some deductions appear to be sound, they are invalid because they violate the rules about **ought** statements.

B If the conclusion of a deduction is a statement of ought, what do you know about the rule at the beginning of the deduction?

A deduction is not valid or correct if the conclusion is an ought statement and the rule at the beginning of the deduction is not an ought statement.

Below are several deductions. Figure out whether each deduction is valid.

- Here's the first deduction:

  Nearly 90 percent of the people preferred beef.
  Beef is available at nearly every supermarket.
  Therefore, you ought to choose beef.

  What kind of statement does the deduction begin with?
  What kind of statement is the conclusion?
  Is the deduction valid?
  Explain.

- Here's another deduction:

  We should stand up for what we believe.
  John believes that the school day should be made longer.
  Therefore, John should stand up for making a longer school day.

  What kind of statement does the deduction begin with?
  Is the deduction valid?
  Explain.

- Here's another deduction:

  Suspected criminals should have fair trials.
  Jake is a suspected criminal.
  Therefore, Jake should have a fair trial.

  What kind of statement does the deduction begin with?
  Is the deduction valid?
  Explain.

- Here's another deduction:

  Aluminum can be recycled.
  Pop cans are made of aluminum.
  Therefore, pop cans should be recycled.

  What kind of statement does the deduction begin with?
  Is the deduction valid?
  Explain.

In the final set of exercises, the students assess the validity of an argument and then decide whether they agree with it. Frequently, students attack an argument if they don't like the conclusion. Conversely, they agree with an argument if they like the conclusion. The purpose of these exercises as shown in the example on the next page is to show students that whether or not you agree with an argument has nothing to do with the validity of that argument.

Many arguments about what we should do begin with **statements of ought.** If the argument draws a conclusion about what somebody ought to do, what do you know about the rule at the beginning of the argument?

Read the argument below.

> One of our most basic beliefs is that we should be fair to all, regardless of race, color, or creed. When we look at the courts, however, we are shocked. The courts are not fair to all. The courts have one standard for the wealthy and another standard for the poor. The courts sentence poor people for committing minor crimes. However, the courts do not treat wealthy people in the same way. If we remain consistent with our basic belief, we must conclude that we should change the courts.

What conclusion does the author draw?

Here are the last two parts of a deduction that is based on the author's argument:

The courts are not fair to all.

Therefore, we should change the courts.

The conclusion is an **ought statement.** So, what do you know about the rule at the beginning of the deduction?

Figure out the missing rule.

Say the whole deduction that summarizes the author's argument.

The argument is valid, but you may not agree with it. Do you agree with the rule that we should be fair to all?

What do you think that rule is supposed to mean?

Note that the students are provided an opportunity to express their views on the unstated **ought** rule. They respond to the question Do you agree with the rule that we should be fair to all? Discussions can become lively, but there are no right or wrong answers. The student either accepts an **ought** proposition or rejects it.

The students also learn about the halo effect: **Just because a person is an expert in one area does not mean that the person is an expert in other areas.** The following example is from Lesson 127 in the Student Book.

 Some arguments are faulty because they do not use good sources of information. They use people who are experts in one field to talk about another field.

Read this argument: Professor Deedee has been with the university for twelve years. He is the chairperson of the English department. He has received four awards for his work. All of us who have worked with him have marveled over how intelligent he is. So, when he tells us that our new storm sewers should be routed near the freeway, we should follow his suggestion.

The argument uses Professor Deedee as a source for what kind of information?

Is Professor Deedee a good source for this information?

For what kind of information would Professor Deedee be a good source?

Biased arguments are introduced in Lesson 126. Beginning with Lesson 128, the students learn about the kind of biased arguments used in advertising. These arguments are purposely designed to give the impression that they say something. Analysis of the arguments shows, however, that these ads do not actually say what they seem to say. The example at right shows part of an exercise from Lesson 132 in the Workbook.

 Read the ads and answer the questions.

- All Miter toys are totally nontoxic. That means that we use paint and other materials that are nonpoisonous. Children playing with Miter toys are totally safe from any possible poisoning caused by paint or glue. If we go to the trouble of making sure that there is no possible way that our toys can poison your children, you can imagine the care we take with every other detail of our toys.

2. Write a sentence that would be in the ad if the ad said that Pure and Fresh mouthwash gets rid of bad breath.

   (Pure and Fresh mouthwash gets rid of bad breath.)

Contradictions

Contradictions start in Lesson 11 with the introduction of this rule: **If a statement is true, a contradiction of that statement is false.** As shown below in Lesson 12, the students are given some facts and statements that contradict those facts. The students indicate why each statement is a contradiction by completing an **if-then** statement.

Assume that this statement is true:

Tom could not drive a car.

Then this statement is a contradiction:

Tom was driving a station wagon down Fifth Street.

Here is why the statement is a contradiction. If Tom could not drive a car, then he could not drive a station wagon down Fifth Street.

• Assume that this statement is true:

Abby swam all morning.

Then this statement is a contradiction:

Abby rode her bike at 10 A.M.

Here is why the statement is a contradiction. If Abby swam all morning, then she could not have ridden her bike at 10 A.M.

• Assume that this statement is true:

Gina loved to eat all vegetables.

Then this statement is a contradiction:

Gina hated to eat broccoli.

Tell why the statement is a contradiction.

If _____, then _____.

To fill in the blanks, start by saying the true statement. Then tell what couldn't also be true.

• Assume that this statement is true:

Jason always sleeps until 9 A.M.

Then this statement is a contradiction:

Jason went fishing today at 6 A.M.

Fill in the blanks to tell why the statement is a contradiction.

If _____, then _____.

Beginning in Lesson 14, the students are shown how to make up **if-then** statements that explain contradictions in passages. The following examples show two exercises presented in Lesson 16, one from the Student Book and the other from the Workbook.

Here's how to find a contradiction in a passage:

  1. Start out assuming that what the speaker says first is true.
  2. Read until you find a contradiction.
  3. Make up an if-then statement that explains the contradiction.

What are the three things you do to find a contradiction in a passage?

 Here s a passage:

> Frank was getting ready for his fishing trip. <u>At 5:30 in the afternoon, he waterproofed his boots</u>. Then he made six sandwiches, filled a jug with hot cocoa, and put everything in a basket. When Frank drove off a few minutes later, the sunrise was turning the sky pink.

1. We assume that the underlined statement is true. Something else the writer says is a contradiction. Circle the contradiction.
2. Make up an if-then statement that explains the contradiction.

_____

_____

_____

_____

_____

Note that in the sample passage, the statement that is assumed to be true is underlined. In later exercises, no words are underlined. The students are required to assume that statements made earlier in the passage are true. The second example shows an exercise from Lesson 38 in the Workbook.

 There are no underlined statements in the passage below. Read the passage. Find a statement that contradicts an earlier statement.

- Underline the statement you assume to be true.
- Circle the contradiction.
- Make up an if-then statement that explains the contradiction.

> I really care about my health. Every morning, I take two vitamin C tablets and one multivitamin tablet. A lot of people don't like to take pills. I'll admit it's difficult to choke down five vitamin pills every morning, but I think it's worth it.

_____

_____

_____

_____

_____

In Lesson 43, the students are presented with statements that contradict what is shown in a picture. In subsequent lessons, similar exercises are done with maps and passages. The following example is from Lesson 43 in the Student Book.

Each square on the map below is five kilometers long and five kilometers wide. Assume that the map is accurate. Examine the map carefully, and then read the statements that follow it. Some of the statements contradict what is shown on the map. For each contradictory statement, tell what the map shows.

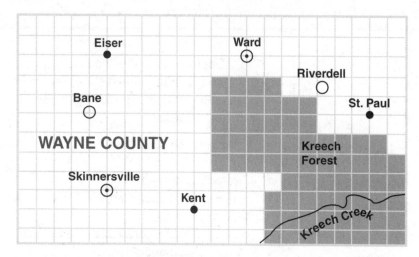

Areas that are shaded like this ▮ are state parks.
The symbol ● means that the city has between 1000 and 5000 people.
The symbol ○ means that the city has between 5000 and 10,000 people.
The symbol ⊙ means that the city has between 10,000 and 50,000 people.

- Statement 1: **The shortest distance from Bane to Kreech Forest is twenty kilometers.**

Does that statement contradict what the map shows?

- Statement 2: **Riverdell is closer to Kreech Forest than Ward is.**

Does that statement contradict what the map shows?

- Statement 3: **The population of Bane is greater than the population of Skinnersville.**

Does that statement contradict what the map shows?

Write **Part D** in the left margin of your paper. Then number it from 1 to 5. Read the statements below. Some of the statements contradict what the map shows.

- Write **contradictory** or **not contradictory** for each statement.
- If a statement contradicts the map, write what the map shows.

1. The shortest distance from Bane to Kreech Forest is twenty kilometers.
2. Riverdell is closer to Kreech Forest than Ward is.
3. The population of Bane is greater than the population of Skinnersville.
4. There are five cities in Wayne County with more than 5000 people.
5. Part of Kreech Creek lies inside Kreech Forest.

Beginning in Lesson 77, the students are presented with an argument, part of which is contradicted by a map, a picture, or a graph. In the following example from Lesson 77, part of the argument is contradicted by the map.

Here's an argument for where to locate a new business:

Hilldale is the best location for new business in Hinker County. Here's why Hilldale is the best choice:

- Hilldale is located at the intersection of Route 5 and Route 30.
- Hilldale is only sixteen kilometers from Benjamin.
- Hilldale is the largest town in Hinker County.
- Hilldale is only fourteen kilometers from Muckster.

When you consider all these reasons, you see that there could not be a more convenient location for a new business.

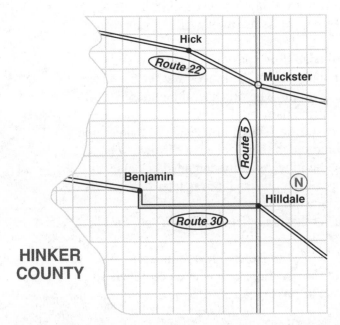

Each square on the map is two kilometers long and two kilometers wide.
The symbol ● means that the city has between 1000 and 5000 people.
The symbol ○ means that the city has between 5000 and 10,000 people.
The symbol ⟨Route 5⟩ means that the road is named Route 5.

Part of the argument is contradicted by the map above. Look at the map and figure out which part.
What does the map show?

Finally, a series of exercises is introduced in which the student must handle contradictory passages. Two accounts of the same situation are presented. The students read both passages and find the major points of disagreement. These exercises sometimes deal with disputes such as the one shown in the following example from Lesson 98.

 A

Written accounts about an event don t always agree. The two accounts below tell about the same event. The accounts contradict each other on an important point. When you read these accounts, look for contradictions.

Passage 1. Last night, the police were on the scene of an accident as it happened. The police car was behind a black sedan at a four-way intersection. A blue sedan failed to stop, skidded through the intersection, and sailed into the black sedan, inflicting serious damage to both vehicles. Almost before the two drivers could step from their cars, Officer Jeffrey Daniels had his ticket pad in hand. Fortunately, nobody was injured; however, Officer Daniels wasted no time in issuing two tickets to Sidney Grapp, driver of the blue vehicle. One ticket was for failing to stop at a stop sign, and the other was for driving without proper control of the vehicle. According to city officials, Officer Daniels now holds the record for issuing tickets quickly. The accident occurred at 9:34 P.M., and the tickets were issued by 9:37 P.M. This record may stand for some time.

Passage 2. Last night, a blue sedan drove past a stop sign. As the sedan crossed the intersection, the driver slammed on the brakes and the car nearly came to a stop before hitting a black sedan. The driver of the blue sedan slowly stepped from his car to assess the damage. He commented that the only damage to the black sedan was a little scratch in the side of the car and a dented hubcap. The driver of the blue sedan then looked at his own vehicle. The front bumper, the grill, and the hood were badly dented. The damages amounted to over $1000. The driver of the blue sedan was later ticketed for $100 because he had failed to stop at a stop sign.

These accounts contradict each other on one big point. What point is that?

Write **Part A** in the left margin of your paper. Then number it from 1 to 12. Answer each question. Some of the questions ask where you found an answer. Write **passage 1, passage 2,** or **passages 1 and 2** for these questions.

1. At what time did the accident take place?
2. Where did you find the answer to question 1?
3. How many dollars worth of damage did the blue sedan suffer?
4. Where did you find the answer to question 3?
5. Which vehicle was at fault?
6. Where did you find the answer to question 5?
7. What parts of the blue sedan were damaged?
8. Where did you find the answer to question 7?
9. Who was in the car behind the black sedan?
10. Where did you find the answer to question 9?
11. How did the police officer set a record?
12. Where did you find the answer to question 11?

A final variation of contradictory passages begins in Lesson 104. This variation was discussed in the section about supporting evidence on page 28 of this guide.

When the students complete the Contradictions exercises, they understand that information that contradicts an argument can come from other arguments, graphs, maps, or pictures. The students also know how to find out which of several contradictory sources is accurate.

Fact Games

The principal goal of the Fact Games is to provide students with sufficient practice to succeed on Mastery Tests of information and vocabulary introduced in the program. Following the Fact Game is an in-program Mastery Test on the same items. Students quickly learn that if they pay attention during the Fact Game, they can get all the items right on the Mastery Test. This demonstration is important to many of the students because they may never have succeeded before on a test. Success often stimulates them to work harder and to begin realizing that they can succeed.

The secret to making the Fact Games successful is tight management. Students should be busy with the games, not talking or acting indifferently. The simplest way to assure that they will be involved is to use points and reinforcement for students (and groups) who perform well.

Introducing the First Fact Game

The instructions following Lesson 15 indicate that the students are to play a Fact Game before they do Lesson 16. You may schedule this game for a time other than the daily reading period.

The instructions for the first game specify that you are to be the monitor and demonstrate with four players how the game is to be played. When demonstrating the game, make sure that you model fast pacing, correct procedures, and the monitor's appropriate responses to the players.

After demonstrating a few rounds of the game, assign the students to permanent groups. Ideally, a group should consist of four players and a monitor. In some situations, you may have to make up a group that consists of three or five players and a monitor. If possible, try to avoid larger groups. Each player in a larger group will receive fewer turns and the management problems of the group will increase.

Do not make the groups homogeneous. Do not place the better performers in one group and the lower performers in another. Rather, mix the students.

Assign monitors who are competent. The monitors should be good readers. Try to assign different monitors each time a Fact Game is played. Tell the monitors their responsibilities. They are to make sure that the players are taking turns, moving to the left. The monitor directs the player who is taking a turn to read the item aloud and answer it. Then the monitor confirms a correct response or gives the correct answer if the item was missed.

The next player does not roll the dice until the preceding player has answered and is told whether the response is correct. (If players are permitted to roll before the item is read and answered, they become so intent on getting ready for their turn that they do not attend to the preceding player's item and the answer.)

Following are procedures for setting up the groups. If possible, provide a table for each group of players. There should be no obstructions that prohibit the monitor from observing the players. The players should not be directly next to the monitor so they can read the answers in the monitor's Workbook. Each player's Workbook should be on the table, opened to the item sheet for the game. The monitor should have a pencil.

For the first game, give each group a pair of dice. The items presented during the game appear in the back of the Workbook. Each game is labeled. The answers appear on another page in the back of the Workbook. For game 1, the items appear on page 427 and the answers appear on page 439.

◆ The monitor is the only person in a group who is permitted to look at the answer page.

◆ The other players take turns. A player rolls the dice, reads the number of dots showing, reads the item that has the same number, and tells the answer.

◆ If the player answers correctly, the monitor makes one tally mark in the box at the top of the player's question sheet.

◆ The dice go to the next player (the player to the left), and that player takes a turn.

Observing the Fact Games

Use the following guidelines when you observe the games.

Reinforce a fast pace. Praise the players who have the dice ready to roll, find the item quickly, read it correctly, and answer correctly. Remind the players that the faster they play, the more points they can earn. A fast pace also ensures that the players will be less likely to argue with the monitor.

Make comments about each group's progress: Look how well you're doing. You've already played three rounds. Comments of this type are important because they let the students know that they are part of a group that is working together.

Do not permit the games to drag. If a group is going slowly, comment on a group that is moving quickly: Wow, this group is really moving. Every player has had five turns already.

Make sure that players are following the rules. After the players have played the game for a few minutes, they may remember what item 5 is or what item 3 is. Therefore, they may attempt to answer the item without first reading the item aloud. Stop players who do not read the item aloud and remind them of the rule: You must **read** the item aloud and **then** answer it. This stipulation is very important. The item a student responds to will help **all** students in the group if the item is read aloud.

Make sure monitors award points only when the answers are correct. For nearly all items, the correct response is phrased in a very specific way, which is indicated in the answer key. If the player's response is not the same as that in the key, the response is incorrect.

If an answer is not correct, the monitor is to read the correct answer aloud. The students are not permitted to argue with the monitor. If they argue, they lose a turn. If they continue to argue, they are removed from the game. The monitors are to raise their hand to signal a problem or a question.

Award bonus points for games that run smoothly and for individual players who receive a certain number of points during the game. For the first game, the specified minimum is more than 10 points; for subsequent games, it is more than 12. Don't make your awards a secret. As you circulate among the groups, announce things like This group is really doing well. If they keep it up, they'll get bonus points for playing the game smoothly.

Stop the game after it has been played for the specified time. The first game is to run for 15 minutes; subsequent games are to run for 20 minutes. You may reduce the time limit to 15 minutes for later games if the group is firm on oral comprehension tasks and Workbook items.

When only 5 minutes of playing time remains, tell the groups Only 5 minutes more. In 5 minutes, the game ends. When the time limit is up, tell the groups to stop: If a player has started a turn, finish that turn. Then the game is over.

Tell each group of players how well they did. Announce which groups receive bonus points for playing the game smoothly. Tell all students who have more than the number of points specified, (10 for the first game, 12 for subsequent games) to stand up. Congratulate them and award bonus points to them.

Mastery Tests

The items selected for the Fact Games appear on Mastery Tests that follow the Fact Games. The items have been selected as those that students typically have trouble learning, especially the new vocabulary tested by these items.

If the Fact Games are successful, a large percentage of the students should get all items correct on the Mastery Tests, and virtually no student should do poorly on these tests. **Note:** Students who get all Mastery Test items correct receive 5 bonus points. This contingency provides an additional incentive for students to perform well on the Fact Games.

The in-program Mastery Tests may seem simple within the context of the activities presented in **Comprehension C;** however, these are actually difficult items, and good performance on them indicates to you, and to the students, that they are successful learners.

Comprehension Placement Test

The **Corrective Reading** Comprehension Placement Test is divided into two parts. Part I is an oral test that is individually administered. It provides an evaluation of important language-comprehension skills that are used in various reading-comprehension activities. All students should be tested on part I. If they perform according to the specified criteria, they are tested on part II. Part II is a written test that may be administered to groups of students.

Preparation

Reproduce one copy of the test for each student and each tester. A reproducible copy appears on pages 66–69 of this guide.

Each tester should become thoroughly familiar with both the presentation procedures and the acceptable responses for the various comprehension items. Tester judgment is called for in evaluating the appropriateness of responses to many items.

Administration

Select a quiet place to administer the test. Students who are to be tested later should not observe or hear another student being tested. You will need a test form for each student.

When administering the test, sit across from the student. Position the test form so that the student cannot see what you are writing on the form.

Fill out the top lines of the test form (student information). Keep the filled-out test form and hand the student a clean copy of the test.

Comprehension Part I

During part I of the Comprehension Placement Test, the student does not do any reading. You present all test items orally; the student responds orally.

Start by presenting the following general instructions. I'm going to ask you some questions. Do your best to answer them. There's no time limit, but if you don't know the answer, tell me and we'll move on to the next item. This test is not designed to grade you. It's designed to help us figure out how we can work with you most effectively.

Present the items in order, starting with item 1. If a student responds incorrectly, circle the response number that follows the item. To help you keep track, you may want to draw a line through the number when the item is answered correctly.

Items 1–3: Divergent Reasoning

These are items involving **same** and **different.** Present the instructions in a normal speaking voice. There are three response numbers for each of these items. For example, if a student names two acceptable ways that a hamburger and an ice-cream cone are different, draw lines through 1a and 1b. If the student does not name a third acceptable way, circle 1c.

You may prompt a student by saying You've named two ways that they're the same. Can you think of another way? If the student does not respond within 10 seconds after the reminder, circle the number and go to the next item.

The responses printed on the test sheet are only samples—not an exhaustive list of appropriate answers. A student's response is appropriate if it (a) expresses how the objects are the same (or how they are different), and (b) has not already been given for the pair of objects.

Note that responses are correct for the **different** items if a student mentions only one of the items. For instance, if the student says the ice-cream cone has a cone, but does not mention the hamburger, the assumption is that the hamburger does not have a cone. Therefore, the response is acceptable.

If you are in doubt about the acceptability of a response, ask the student to give a different one. For example, the student responds to item 1 by indicating that a hamburger is hot, that a hamburger has a bun, and that an ice-cream cone is cold. The last response is questionable because it is the opposite of the first response. Say Can you name another way that an ice-cream cone is different from a hamburger? Score the student's response to your question.

Items 4–6: Analogies

Item 4 is an analogy that tells where objects are found (or where the objects typically operate). Any response that accurately tells where is acceptable. For example, *lake, stream, fishing hole, ocean, aquarium,* and *under lily pads,* are acceptable.

Item 5 tells which class each object is in. Acceptable responses include *cold-blooded things, animals, food,* and *living things.*

Item 6 deals with parts of objects. Acceptable responses include *fins, tails, gills, scales, eyes,* and *teeth.*

Items 7–9: Recitation Behavior

These items test statement-repetition skill. The student receives as many as three tries at repeating the statement. You say the statement and tell the student to repeat it. If the student says exactly what you say, draw a line through the response number for that trial. If the student does not say exactly what you say, circle the number. As soon as the student repeats the statement correctly, go to the next item.

For example, if the student correctly says the statement in item 8 on the first try, draw a line through 8a and go to item 9. If the student does not say the statement correctly on the first try, circle 8a and say Let's try it again. Repeat the statement. Continue until the student has said the item correctly or until you have circled 8c.

Students must say the words clearly so they are not confused with other words. Watch for word substitutions, word omissions, and the omission of word endings—for example, saying "twenty-seven" instead of "twenty-seventh" in item 8. On the second and third try, you may emphasize the part of the sentence the student said incorrectly.

Items 10–15: Basic Information

These items test general information. For items 11 and 14, there is more than one acceptable response. For the others, however, only one answer is acceptable.

Items 16–19: Deductions

These items assess the student's ability to use deductions. Nonsense words are used in item 19. If students object to the nonsense words, remind them You can still answer the questions even if you don't know the meaning of some of the words.

Students are not required to use the precise words specified for the items; however, they should give acceptable substitutions.

Items 20–22: Divergent Reasoning

These items test the student's ability to use concepts related to **true** and **false.** Items 20 and 21 deal with descriptions that are true of some things, while item 22 deals with a contradiction (one part must be false if the other part is true).

Note that item 20c is to be presented only if the student answers 20b correctly. If the response to 20b is incorrect, circle 20b and 20c. Then go on to item 21.

Placement

Total the student's errors by counting every circled response number. Enter the total in the score blank at the beginning of the test form. Then determine the placement of the student.

PLACEMENT SCHEDULE: COMPREHENSION PART I

Total Errors	Comprehension Placement
31 or more	Place in a beginning language program, e.g., *Language for Learning*
27 to 30	Provisional placement in Level A, Lesson A*
17 to 26	Level A, Lesson A
12 to 16	Level A, Lesson 1
9 to 11	Level B1, Lesson 1
0 to 8	Administer part II

*Some students who perform in this range may perform well on Lessons A through E of Level A. If not, place them in a beginning language program.

Comprehension Part II

Part II of the Comprehension Placement Test requires students to read silently and write answers. Students should not be helped with decoding or with answers. Part II may be administered to groups of students.

Scoring

Each incorrect response counts as 1 error. If students correctly underline only part of the specified group of words in section A or B, score $\frac{1}{2}$ error.

Answer Guide

A. Words underlined:
 little plants that grow in twinglers wapdumpos
B. Words underlined:
 a small kerchief around his wrist drosling
C. 1000 gallons
 1100 gallons
 The price of milk will go up.
D.

a. 8	e. 20	i. 4
b. 1	f. 2	j. 13
c. 19	g. 3	k. 7
d. 6	h. 10	l. 16

PLACEMENT SCHEDULE: COMPREHENSION PART II

Total Errors	Comprehension Placement
$5\frac{1}{2}$ or more	Level B1, Lesson 1
2 to 5	Level C, Lesson 1
0 to $1\frac{1}{2}$	Too advanced for *Corrective Reading* series

Name _____ Class _____ Date _____

School _____ Tester _____

COMPREHENSION Part I Errors _____   Comprehension placement _____

COMPREHENSION Part II Errors _____   Comprehension placement _____

COMPREHENSION Part I

(Read to the student:)   (Circle Errors)

1. Name three ways that an ice-cream cone is different from a hamburger.
   One is hot. A hamburger has a bun.   1a
   One is sweet. One has meat. An ice-   1b
   cream cone has a cone. (and so forth)   1c

2. Name three ways that an ice-cream cone is like a hamburger.
   They are food. Each is bigger than an   2a
   ant. Both have parts. Both are   2b
   purchased. You eat them. (and so forth)   2c

3. Name three ways that a tree is the same as a cat.
   They are alive. Each is bigger than an   3a
   ant. Both die. They reproduce. Both   3b
   have coverings. (and so forth)   3c

4. Finish this sentence:
   An **airplane** is to **air** as a **fish** is to . . .
   Water, a lake, an ocean, etc.   4

5. Finish this sentence:
   An **airplane** is to **vehicles** as a **fish** is to . . .
   Animals, food, etc.   5

6. Finish this sentence:
   An **airplane** is to **wings** as a **fish** is to . . .
   Fins   6

I'll say some sentences. After I say a sentence, you try to say it exactly as I said it.

7. Here's a new sentence: 7a
   The man on first base was not very   7b
   fast. Say it.   7c

8. Here's a new sentence: 8a
   It was March twenty-seventh,   8b
   nineteen sixty-five. Say it.   8c

9. Here's a new sentence: 9a
   Some of the people who live in   9b
   America are illiterate. Say it.   9c

10. How many weeks are in a year?
    52   10

(Read to the student:)   (Circle Errors)

11. Listen: It has four wooden legs and a seat and a back. What is it?
    Couch or chair   11

12. Listen: We celebrate this day every year because it's the first day of the new year. What date is that?
    January 1 or the first of January (In countries other than the United States, substitute a comparable local holiday.)   12

13. Say the days of the week.
    Students may start with any day of the week, but the days must be recited in order.   13

14. What is a synonym for **sad?**
    Unhappy, downcast   14

15. One season of the year is summer.
    Name the three other seasons.
    Fall, winter, spring (can be given in
    any order)   15

(Read to the student:)   (Circle Errors)

16. Listen: If a dog is green, it has five legs.
    a. Pam's dog is green. What else do you know about it?
    Idea: It has five legs.   16a
    b. Jim has something with five legs. Is it green?
    Idea: Maybe, or I don't know.   16b

17. Listen: Some lobsters are red.
    a. Tony has a lobster. Is it red?
    Idea: Maybe, or I don't know.   17a
    b. Mary has a lobster. Is it red?
    Idea: Maybe, or I don't know.   17b

18. Listen: No brick walls have paint specks. Jerome has a brick wall. What else do you know about it?
    Idea: It doesn't have paint specks.   18

19. Here's a rule. It has silly words, but you can still answer the questions.
    Listen: All lerbs have pelps.
    Listen again: All lerbs have pelps.
    a. Tom has a lerb. What do you know about his lerb?
    Idea: It has pelps.   19a
    b. What would you look for to find out if something is a lerb?
    Idea: Pelps.   19b

(Read to the student:)   (Circle Errors)

20. Listen: It is used to write with.
    a. Is that true of a pencil?
    Yes   20a
    b. Is that true of only a pencil?
    No   20b
    (Present 20c only if 20b is answered correctly.)
    c. Name two other things it is true of.
    Pen, crayon, chalk, etc.   20c

21. Listen: It is a farm animal that has four legs, goes "moo," and gives milk.
    a. Is that true of a cow?
    Yes   21a
    b. Is that true of only a cow?
    Yes   21b

22. Listen to this statement and tell me what's wrong with it.
    He was fifteen years old and his younger sister was eighteen years old.
    Idea: His younger sister is not younger than he is.   22

COMPREHENSION Part II

A. They planted wapdumpos, little plants that grow in twinglers.

The sentence tells the meaning of a word. Which word? _____
Underline the part of the sentence that tells what the word means.

B. His drosling, a small kerchief around his wrist, was made of silk and grosplops.

The sentence tells the meaning of a word. Which word? _____
Underline the part of the sentence that tells what the word means.

C. Here's a rule: When the demand is greater than the supply, prices go up.

Digo Dairy sells 1000 gallons of milk every day. Digo Dairy has orders for 1100 gallons of milk every day.

How much is the supply of milk? _____

How much is the demand for milk? _____

What is going to happen to the price of milk at Digo Dairy? _____

_____

D. For each word in the left column, write the number of the word or phrase from the right column that means the same thing.

a.	currency	_____	**1.**	all at once	
b.	suddenly	_____	**2.**	silently	
			3.	movable	
c.	ambiguous	_____	**4.**	changed	
d.	hesitated	_____	**5.**	contended	
			6.	paused	
e.	exhibited	_____	**7.**	plan	
			8.	money	
f.	quietly	_____	**9.**	rate	
			10.	rules	
g.	portable	_____	**11.**	vehicles	
			12.	general	
h.	regulations	_____	**13.**	fittingly	
i.	converted	_____	**14.**	clean	
			15.	clear	
j.	appropriately	_____	**16.**	answer	
			17.	responsible	
k.	strategy	_____	**18.**	gradually	
			19.	unclear	
l.	response	_____	**20.**	showed	
			21.	hidden	
			22.	caused	
			23.	slowly	

Scope and Sequence Chart

The Scope and Sequence Chart provides an overview of the skills taught in **Comprehension C.** The skills are divided into five principal areas: Organizing Information, Operating on Information, Using Sources of Information, Communicating Information, and Using Information for Directions. The chart indicates which lessons offer practice in a given skill.

ORGANIZATION INFORMATION

Main Idea
Outlining
Specific-General
Morals
Visual-Spatial Organization

OPERATING ON INFORMATION

Deductions   1
Basic Evidence   1
Argument Rules
Ought Statements
Contradictions

USING SOURCES OF INFORMATION

Basic Comprehension Passages
Words or Deductions
Maps, Pictures, Graphs
Supporting Evidence

COMMUNICATING INFORMATION

Definitions
Combining Sentences   1
Editing   1
Meaning from Context

USING INFORMATION FOR DIRECTIONS

Writing Directions   4
Filling out Forms
Identifying Contradictory Directions

FACT GAMES

MASTERY TESTS

In-Program Mastery Tests
Mid-Program Mastery Tests
End-of-Program Mastery Tests

LESSONS 1–140

61   140
91   140
112   140
121   140
84   140

140
140
42   140
91   140
11   140

15   58
64   140
33   140
38   140

17   140
140
140
104   140

140
11   140
25   140

| 15 | 30 | 45 | 60 | 75 | 90 | 105 | 120 | 135 |

| 15 | 30 | 45 | 60 | 75 | 90 | 105 | 120 | 135 |

70

140

Behavioral Objectives

The following chart gives specific information for each skill taught in **Comprehension C.** Three columns of information are provided. The **Behavioral objective** column details the kind of performance that can be expected from a student who has mastered the skill. The column headed **The student is asked to** describes the tasks the student performs in order to master the skill. The **Lessons** column shows the lessons in which the skill appears.

Organizing Information

Main Idea

BEHAVIORAL OBJECTIVE	The student is asked to	LESSONS
Given a written passage, the student will be able to identify the main idea.	Identify the main idea of a passage	61–140
Given a series of written passages, the student will be able to identify the passage that tells more about the subject, identify the main idea, and answer questions about the passage.	Determine which passage tells more about a subject; choose the main idea; answer questions about the passage	108–138

Outlining

Given a written passage, the student will be able to identify the main idea and outline the major points contained in the passage.	Lists the main idea and the points that fall under it	91–140

Specific-General

BEHAVIORAL OBJECTIVE	The student is asked to	LESSONS
Given a sentence, the student will be able to modify an identified part of the sentence to make it more specific in content or general in content.	1) Change an underlined part to become more general; to become more specific; 2) Rewrite a sentence to become more general; to become more specific	112–119 121–124

Morals

Given a written passage, the student will be able to identify the main idea and outline the major points contained in the passage.	Lists the main idea and the points that fall under it	91–140
Given a written passage, the student will be able to determine and write the moral of the passage.	Determine and write the moral of the passage	121–135

Visual-Spatial Organization

Given a blank outline chart and a set of facts, the student will be able to fill in the appropriate information to complete the chart.	Study the facts and fill in the chart	84–140

Operating on Information

Deductions

BEHAVIORAL OBJECTIVE	The student is asked to	LESSONS
Given a rule statement that involves *all, some, part,* or *every,* the student will be able to complete the deduction.	Complete a deduction that involves *all, some, part,* or *every*	1–138
Given a pictured diagram, the student will be able to complete the deduction based on the information given in the diagram.	Complete a deduction based on the diagram	1–140
Given a rule statement and additional evidence, the student will be able to write a conclusion.	Write a conclusion for each piece of evidence	75–132

Basic Evidence

Given two facts and an outcome statement, the student will be able to identify which fact explains why the outcome occurred.	Identify which of two facts explains a specific outcome	1–4
Given a series of written circumstances and a set of facts, the student will be able to identify which circumstance is *relevant* or *irrelevant* to a fact.	Identify which circumstance is *relevant* or *irrelevant* to a fact	5–138
Given two sentences, the student will be able to find evidence to support or contradict a conclusion.	Find evidence to support or contradict a conclusion; write the evidence	31–139

Argument Rules

BEHAVIORAL OBJECTIVE	The student is asked to	LESSONS
Given a passage, the student will be able to identify the conclusion intended by the author and verbally explain how the argument is faulty.	Identify the conclusion intended by the author; tell what rule the argument breaks; explain how to prove the argument is faulty	42–140
Given written information, the student will be able to identify a good source of information and verbally explain the kind of information the source would be useful for.	Identify a good source of information; tell about the kinds of information the source would be useful for	124–139
The student will be able to identify a biased argument and verbally explain why it is biased.	Identify a biased argument and explain why it is biased	126–139
Given a written ad, the student will be able to identify the implication and write a sentence that states what the ad implies.	Identify the implication of an ad; write a sentence that states what the ad implies	128–138

Ought Statements

Given a written statement, the student will be able to explain whether it is a *statement of fact* or a *statement of ought*.	Tell whether the statement is a *statement of fact* or a *statement of ought*	96–135
The student will be able to write a complete *ought* deduction based on a given argument.	Write a complete *ought* deduction based on a given argument	128–130

Using Sources of Information

Basic Comprehension Passages

BEHAVIORAL OBJECTIVE	The student is asked to	LESSONS
Given a story, the student will be able to read and answer specific comprehension questions about the story.	Read the story and answer questions about it	15–92

Words or Deductions

Given a written passage, the student will be able to identify the main idea and outline the major points contained in the passage.	Lists the main idea and the points that fall under it	91–140
Given a written passage, the student will be able to read it, answer questions, and explain whether the questions are answered by specific words within the passage or by a deduction.	Read the passage; answer comprehension questions; tell whether the question is answered by words in the passage or by a deduction	64–138

Maps, Pictures, Graphs

Given a map, the student will be able to read it and answer specific questions about it.	Read the map and answer questions about it	33–41
Given a picture, the student will be able to answer specific questions about it.	Study the picture and answer questions about it	39–42

Maps, Pictures, Graphs *cont.*

BEHAVIORAL OBJECTIVE	The student is asked to	LESSONS
Given a picture, map, or graph, the student will be able to determine whether a given statement contradicts what is actually shown.	Determine whether the statement contradicts a picture, map, or graph; tell what is actually shown	39–42
Given a graph, the student will be able to interpret and answer questions about it.	Read the graph and answer questions about it	67–74

Supporting Evidence

Given a fact, the student will be able to indicate the reference book most appropriate for finding evidence that supports the fact.	Determine the best source of information (an atlas, dictionary, or encyclopedia) that supports the given fact; name the kinds of information found in the reference books	31–122

Contradictory Passages

Given some facts and statements that contradict those facts, the student will indicate why each statement is a contradiction by completing an *if-then* statement.	Complete an *if-then* statement to explain a contradiction	11–27
Given a passage with underlined contradictory information, the student will be able to make up an *if-then* statement that explains the contradiction.	Make up an *if-then* statements that explains the contradiction	14–27

Contradictory Passages *cont.*

BEHAVIORAL OBJECTIVE	The student is asked to	LESSONS
Given a passage, the student will be able to identify the contradiction and explain it with an *if-then* statement.	Name the contradiction and explain it with an *if-then* statement.	38–137
Given a passage and several statements, the student will determine which statements contradict the facts in the passage.	Determine if each statement contradicts a fact in the passage.	51–134
Given two passages that contradict each other on an important event, the student will be able to identify the major points of disagreement.	Read both passages and tell how the passages contradict each other.	98–136

Communicating Information

Definitions

BEHAVIORAL OBJECTIVE	The student is asked to	LESSONS
Given a sentence that contains a vocabulary word, the student will be able to tell what the word means and substitute the word for its synonym.	1) Tell the definition of the following words: hesitate, opportunity, ambiguous, redundant, convert, currency, regulation, restrict, replete, extraneous, response, devise, appropriate, strategy, phenomenon, anxiety, exhibit, usually, occasionally, rarely, contend, valid, motive, conceal, data, especially, particularly 2) use the vocabulary word in a sentence by substituting the word for its synonym; 3) write a new sentence.	18–138

Communicating Information cont

Definitions

BEHAVIORAL OBJECTIVE	The student is asked to	LESSONS
Given a series of new words and their definitions to read and study, the student will be able to edit paragraphs, substituting words in the passage with new vocabulary words.	1) Read and study the new words and their definitions; 2) edit paragraphs by substituting words in the passage with new vocabulary words: catastrophe, inquiries, overpopulated, temporary, wildlife, affirmed, audibly, imitation, remote, clarity, cautious, sorrow, rogue, sanctioned, scrupulous, somnolent, indolent, lethal, preceding, vital, extrovert, genius, subsequent, tightwad, emphatically, independent, proximity	70–130

Combining Sentences

Given two sentences with common parts, the student will be able to combine them using *but, however, so, and, therefore, who, which.*	Combine pairs of sentences using: but however so therefore who which	5–140 8–140 17–140 17–140 17–140 44–140 44–140

Editing

Given a paragraph with the verbs *is, are, was,* and *were* used incorrectly, the student will be able to recognize and correct the errors.	Find and correct errors with: *was—were* *is—are* *has—have*	21–136 21–124 41–108

Editing *cont.*

BEHAVIORAL OBJECTIVE	The student is asked to	LESSONS
Given a sentence, the student will be able to identify the redundant part and explain why it is redundant.	Identify the redundant part of a sentence; tell why it is redundant.	76–139

Meaning from Content

Given a passage with an underlined word, the student will be able to tell from the context of the passage what the underlined word means.	Determine the meaning of the underlined word from the context of the passage; circle the synonym; identify a sentence that contradicts a wrong meaning.	95–137
Given a sentence with two possible meanings, the student will be able to analyze the sentence for the unintended meaning.	Name the two possible meanings of the sentence; identify the intended meaning; identify which word is involved in the two meanings.	104–134
Given a paragraph to read, the student will be able to explain why something happened.	Write the clue that suggests why something happened; name two ways that the clue could cause the outcome.	131–138

Using Information for Directions

Writing Directions

BEHAVIORAL OBJECTIVE	The student is asked to	LESSONS
Given a diagram and some prompt words, the student will be able to focus on writing instructions that tell *what* to make and *where* to make it.	Write step-by-step directions for drawing a diagram by: 1) Completing partial directions; 2) using prompt words.	3–12 9–137

Filling Out Forms

Given factual information, the student will be able to complete various forms.	Fill out a variety of forms.	11–139

Identifying Contradictory Directions

Given a diagram and a list of instructions, the student will be able to explain which instruction a diagram contradicts and draw a new diagram that is consistent with the instructions.	1) Tell what instruction a diagram contradicts; 2) Draw a new diagram that follows the instructions	25–53 25–133

Fact Games and In-Program Mastery Tests

There are nine Fact Games and Mastery Tests formats in **Comprehension C.** A Fact Game and Mastery Test are presented after a series of lessons have been taught. The Fact Games and Mastery Tests incorporate the skills and concepts presented in previous lessons. A list of the Fact Games and Mastery Tests, fact or skill covered, and a schedule for presenting the Fact Games and Mastery Tests is provided below.

Fact Game/ Mastery Test	Fact or Skill Covered	Schedule
1	Writing Directions Basic Evidence Sentence Combinations (*however, but*) Editing Deductions	After Lesson 15
2	Basic Evidence Combining Sentences (*so, therefore, and*) Definitions	After Lesson 30
3	Deductions Basic Evidence Supporting Evidence Editing Combining Sentences Definitions	After Lesson 45
4	Basic Evidence Combining Sentences Contradictory Passages Deductions	After Lesson 60
5	Basic Evidence Maps, Pictures, Graphs Definitions Sentence Combinations Argument Rules	After Lesson 75
6	Combining Sentences Argument Rules Basic Evidence Definitions Supporting Evidence Sentence Combinations	After Lesson 90

Fact Game/ Mastery Test	Fact or Skill Covered	Schedule
7	Supporting Evidence Editing Definitions Ought Statements Maps, Pictures, Graphs	After Lesson 105
8	Supporting Evidence Contradictory Passages Maps, Pictures, Graphs Definitions Specific-General Combining Sentences	After Lesson 120
9	Maps, Pictures, Graphs Basic Evidence Sentence Combining Supporting Evidence Argument Rules	After Lesson 135

Skills Profile Chart

The Skills Profile Chart can be used to record an individual student's mastery of each skill taught in **Comprehension C.** The chart summarizes the skills presented in the program and provides space for indicating when a student has mastered each skill. One copy of the chart should be made for each student in the class.

Organizing Information

SKILLS	LESSON RANGE	DATE MASTERED
Main Idea Identifies the main idea of a passage	61–140	
Determines which passage tells more about a subject; chooses the main idea; answers questions	108–138	
Outlining Lists the main idea and the points that fall under it	91–140	
Specific-General Changes an underlined part to become more general; to become more specific	112–119	
Rewrites a sentence to become more general; to become more specific	121–124	
Morals Determines and writes the moral of a passage	121–135	
Visual-Spatial Organization Fills in a chart	84–140	

Operating on Information

SKILLS	LESSON RANGE	DATE MASTERED
Deductions Completes a deduction that involves, *all, some, part, every*	1–138	
Completes a deduction based on a diagram	1–140	
Given a rule and some evidence, writes a conclusion for each piece of evidence	75–132	
Basic Evidence Identifies which of two facts explains a specific outcome	1–4	
Identifies which circumstances are relevant or irrelevant to a fact	5–138	
Finds evidence to support or contradict a conclusion and writes the evidence	31–139	
Argument Rules Identifies the conclusion intended by the author; tells what rule the argument breaks; explains how to prove the argument is faulty	42–140	
Identifies a good source of information; tells about the kinds of information the source would be useful for	124–139	
Identifies a biased argument; tells why it is biased	126–139	
Identifies the implication of an ad; writes a sentence that states what the ad implies	128–138	
Ought Statements Tells whether a statement is a *statement of fact or a statement* of ought	96–135	
Writes a complete ought deduction based on a given argument	128–130	

Using Information for Directions

SKILLS	LESSON RANGE	DATE MASTERED
Writing Directions Writes step-by-step directions for drawing a diagram by: completing partial directions using prompt words	 3–12 9–137	
Filling Out Forms Fills out a variety of forms	11–139	
Identifying Contradictory Directions Tells what instruction a diagram contradicts	25–53	

Using Sources of Infomation

SKILLS	LESSON RANGE	DATE MASTERED
Basic Comprehension Passages Reads the story and answers questions	15–92	
Words or Deductions Reads a passage; answers comprehension questions; tells whether the question is answered by words in the passage or a deduction	64–138	
Maps, Pictures, Graphs Reads a map and answers questions	33–41	
Studies a picture and answers questions	39–42	
Determines if a statement contradicts a picture, map, graph; tells what is actually shown	41–139	
Reads a graph and answers questions	67–74	
Supporting Evidence Determines the best source of information; encyclopedia, atlas, dictionary; names kinds of information found in these references	31–122	
Contradictory Passages Uses an *if-then* statement to explain a contradiction	11–27	
Writes the statement that contradicts the underlined statement	14–27	
Names the contradiction and explains it with an *if-then* statement	38–137	
Determines if a statement contradicts a passage	51–134	
Tells how two passages contradict each other	98–136	

Communicating Information

SKILLS	LESSON RANGE	DATE MASTERED
Combining Sentences Combines pairs of sentences using the following words: but	 5–140	
however	8–140	
so	17–140	
and	17–140	
therefore	17–140	
who	44–140	
which	44–140	
Editing Finds and corrects errors with was—were	 21–136	
is—are	21–124	
has—have	41–108	
Identifies the redundant part of a sentence; tells why it's redundant	76–139	

Communicating Information

SKILLS	LESSON RANGE	DATE MASTERED
Meaning from Context Determines meaning from context: circles for synonym: identifies a sentence that contradicts a wrong meaning fenestration, magnanimous, notorious, malapropos, panache, ebullient, uncouth, penurious, fubsy, niggling, malign, interrogation, tenacious, loquacious, unctuous, illusion, fallacious, fecund, deprecate, extol, exonerate, innuendo, ignominious, excruciating, fortitude, obliterate, diligent, aesthetic	95–137	
Names the two possible meanings of a sentence and identifies the intended meaning; identifies which word is involved in the two meanings	104–134	
Writes the clue that suggests why something happened; names two ways that the clue could cause the outcome	131–138	
Definitions Tells the definition of the following words; uses the vocabulary word in a sentence by substituting the word for its synonym or filling in a blank; writes the new sentence hesitate, opportunity, ambiguous, redundant, convert, currency, regulation, restrict, replete, extraneous, response, devise, appropriate, strategy, phenomenon, anxiety, exhibit, usually, occasionally, rarely, contend, valid, motive, conceal, data, especially, particularly	18–138	
Reads and studies words (and their definitions) that appear in editing exercises catastrophe, inquiries, coverpopulated, temporary, wildlife, affirmed, audibly, imitation, remote, clarity, cautious, sorrow, rogue, sanctioned, scrupulous, somnolent, indolent, lethal, preceding, vital, extrovert, genius, subsequent, tightwad, emphatically, independent, proximity	70–130	

TEACHER'S RECORD CHART

Student's Name

LESSON